MAN AND THE COMPUTER

Ashley Montagu and Samuel S. Snyder

FIRST EDITION

AUERBACH®
publishers

philadelphia
new york
london

AUERBACH Publishers Inc.,
Philadelphia, 1972

Library of Congress Catalog Card Number: 72-86235
International Standard Book Number: 0-87769-146-0

First Printing

Printed in the United States of America

Library of Congress Cataloging in Publication Data

Montagu, Ashley, 1905–
    Man and the computer.

    Includes bibliographical references.
    1. Computers and civilization. 2. Electronic
digital computers. I. Snyder, Samuel S., 1911–
joint author. II. Title.
QA76.5.M55 1973   301.24'3   72-86235
ISBN 0-87769-146-0

To the memory of Percy W. Bridgman

Contents

Preface

The computer is one of the most exciting technological developments of the modern age. A certain amount of mystique and quite a bit of mythology have already grown up about it: The computer will solve all our problems. It will become a Frankenstein and either enslave or destroy us. It is better than the human brain, Man's future is imperilled by the computer, and so on.

It is the purpose of this book to sift the wheat from the chaff and to present the facts about the computer in such a manner that every reader—be he a computer expert, a computer user, employer, worker, student, or government official—may be able to understand exactly what a computer is, what it can and what it cannot do, and what the citizen can do about seeing to it that it becomes an instrument for the enlargement of man's welfare rather than a negative influence.

Since the computer is such a versatile instrument and the role it is already playing will increasingly affect our lives, a knowledge of what the computer represents and is capable of doing has become really quite indispensable.

The authors hope that they have successfully supplied that knowledge and that the reader will go on from that position to the realization that the meaning of a word is the action it produces.

Our special thanks to Mr. Michel Feuche for his contribution in preparing our manuscript.

Ashley Montagu
Samuel S. Snyder

August 1972

1

Living with the Ultimate Weapon

The first tool ever made by man has long been lost to us. We do not know whether this artifact, crafted nearly a million years ago, was a bone, a stick, or a large pebble. What counts is that it was the first conscious extension of man's powers beyond the strength of muscles and the slash of tooth and claw. It altered the relationship of man to his environment as nothing had ever done before (and possibly not since), and thus could truly be called the "ultimate weapon," the first of a long succession.

There have been many "ultimate weapons" since. Some were transient, such as the crossbow, banned by a medieval pope because it made war too horrible. Others were more potent, such as the steam engine, which made possible the Industrial Revolution. Each of them, however, has deeply affected our relations with our fellow men and to the world we live in. We have perpetually had to learn and relearn how to live with the Ultimate Weapon.

We are now faced with a new ultimate weapon. This is the computer whose potential impact may surpass that of all of man's earlier devices. Many deplore the computer and some even fear it as more monster than machine. Whatever we think of it, however, we must adjust to it. This does not imply resignation, but rather that we must

1

understand the true nature of this latest of man's inventions and learn how its powers can be combined with our own abilities to be used to the best advantage of humanity.

This book is therefore intended to examine the computer and the relationship of computers to mankind. It will also dwell on the question of whether the computer now truly is, or whether any of the preceding devices ever really were, the ultimate weapon—or whether that terrible distinction has not always belonged to their creator, man himself.

THE COMPUTER IMPACT

A major preoccupation of speechwriters and the press often seems to be the devising of clever labels with which to tag each new decade of this century. Thus, we have had (for good reasons) the Roaring Twenties, the Fighting Forties, the Fabulous Fifties, and the recently concluded Soaring Sixties. This decade is as yet untagged, but a label for it has been proposed by Harold S. Geneen, president and chairman of International Telephone and Telegraph Company. The period, he suggests, should be known as the "Insatiable Seventies." This name would truly reflect the ever greater eagerness of the American people to improve their standard of living further, to obtain more convenience and luxuries, and to enjoy better accommodations and additional leisure.

Such desires are probably common to all decades. For nearly two centuries, western man has looked to technology to improve his lot and safeguard him from the consequences of his past mistakes (and perhaps give him the opportunity to make new ones). But society's avid desires may never have seemed so realistic as today with the awesome powers of the computer at its disposal, while automation spreads at a rate that still leaves many of us gasping. However, as the term *insatiable* implies, a tinge of guilt, a feeling that some degree of self-control may be lacking, may well accompany these desires for personal advantage. It seems obvious that these desires can be fulfilled only by further expanding the role of computers in our lives— and many of us are not at all sure that this is a good thing.

There are at least two major reasons why computers have so excited the public imagination and aroused such ambivalent feelings of fear and hope:

We have been experiencing the impact of computers for more than a decade, and that impact has turned out to be far greater than we had conceived, and yet it has been strangely elusive and frustrating.

We know that no matter how great the impact of computers has been to date, it is as nothing to what it will be in the future—and we cannot readily see or control how computers will affect us or what they will finally do to us.

The computer's impact has been all the greater in that it has come so swiftly. It did not seem as though it would at first. The device was first developed in 1946, but for several years it was widely held that the nation's requirements would be for at most about 200 of the "giant brains" (as the press then delighted in calling the machines). In fact, the number of computers in operation did not pass the 1,000 mark until the second half of the 1950s, and there were still fewer than 5,000 installed by 1960. Since then, the situation has changed explosively. By 1970, there were over 70,000 computers in the United States alone, and nearly that many were installed in other countries. At this writing, the number of domestic computer installations has soared to over 80,000, and will top 100,000 before 1975.

There are no previous examples of a technology finding such wide acceptance within so brief a period. In a recent survey of people's attitudes toward computers, 91 percent of those surveyed agreed that computers and their uses are affecting the lives of all of us.[1] That their overall response was positive was borne out by the 75 percent of respondents who felt that computers will improve our lives, and the 86 percent who felt that computers will create more leisure time. No other impact of technology has been so deeply or quickly experienced or has had such a pervasive effect.

From the very first, the ability of computers to process huge amounts of information, perform endless calculations, and solve complex problems—all with eye-blinking rapidity—found applications in defense and all areas of science and engineering. Today, computers are routinely used for tasks ranging from missile guidance to scientific research and the control of entire factories to the design of new brassiere styles (surprisingly, missile guidance is a relatively simple job, while brassiere design requires the solution of difficult problems of stress analysis).

[1] *Time* Magazine, Time, Inc., and American Federation of Information Processing Societies, Inc., "A National Survey of the Public's Attitudes toward Computers," 1972.

But this is not all; use of the computer has not been restricted to defense, science, engineering, and industry. It has also been increasingly used in business and public administration—in all of those areas where we feel the computer's impact as individuals, rather than as managers or employees enjoying the benefits of computerized efficiency. It is in this area, the one that is, after all, of prime importance to us all, that the computer and its impact have come to be regarded with increasing ambivalence.

STRIKING A BALANCE

The computer's impact on our personal lives has been great. It has been as pervasive and as evident as our latest computer-printed bank statement or electric bill. There is hardly any of our routine transactions that is not now computerized—from making a credit card purchase to subscribing to a magazine to the cashing of a paycheck. Insurance firms, banks, government (starting with the Internal Revenue Service), stores, suppliers of all kinds, even churches and synagogues, use computers and fill our mailboxes with computer-produced documents, crammed together with computer-produced junk mail.

Great as the computer's impact on our lives has become, we frequently find it to be as superficial and unsatisfying as the unwanted junk mail the computer generates. For us as individuals, rather than as corporate users, the computer seldom turns out to be a marvelously useful device with which we can interact to have it do our bidding. Too often this interaction is limited to our protesting inaccurate computer-produced bills. This is not an uncommon occurrence. Approximately 47 percent of survey respondents felt that computers often make mistakes in processing bills. In addition, 34 percent said that they have had problems "because of a computer," with faulty billings being the cause in over half the cases.

It may even seem as though our problems stemming from faulty computer billings only really begin with our protests. These are frequently met by bland computer-produced letters assuring us that all will be corrected and made well, but nevertheless the same inaccurate bills are mailed out month after month—accompanied by ever more pointed computer-produced reminders and dunning notices. The computer with all its powers then appears to have been set to work against us with unswerving, moronic persistence. It sometimes seems a wonder that more people do not join the "do not fold, staple, or muti-late" brigade, as they become convinced that the computer provides yet another means of duping them—that "computer mistakes" are really made by the people who use computers, and that many com-panies blame computers for mistakes made by their own people. These beliefs were held, respectively, by 81 and 77 percent of those surveyed.

Obviously, under such circumstances, the computer often ap-pears as a dehumanized, dehumanizing agent of "them" against "us." It hardly seems a likely agent for implementing Marshall McLuhan's famous statement that "*They* has become *We*." These feelings are the direct opposite of those expressed by superoptimists not so many years ago, that computers would help bring about quick and effective solu-tions to most of society's problems. They are also probably just as wrong because the issues involved are too complex for hasty, emo-tional judgments. Indications that the truth lies somewhere between the two poles come, paradoxically, from the failure to come true of many major predictions made about the computer and its effects.

One of the predictions that has most emphatically—and most happily—not worked out is that of "technological unemployment." Automation, the theory went, would, with its superior efficiency, take over all tasks, eating up jobs and driving men out of work. Factory payrolls would be decimated, while, in business, not only clerks but also middle management would be eliminated and replaced by elec-tronic black boxes. Nothing of the sort has happened. Automated fac-tories manned by handfuls of technicians have become common, and the computer is a routine tool of business—but blue-collar employment remains high, clerks are in tight supply, and middle managers are far more numerous today than they were in the 1950s when the predic-tion was made.

Technological unemployment did not come about because new technologies are jobmakers, not job-breakers. Thus 49 percent of those surveyed had held jobs requiring either direct or indirect con-tact with a computer, with 30 percent currently holding such posi-tions. In addition, 15 percent felt that their jobs required some knowl-edge of computing, while 7 percent worked directly with computers. It is estimated that the establishment of a sizable, still expanding computer industry and community has resulted in the creation of over 3 million jobs. Naturally, many tasks, mainly dull, repetitive ones, have been phased out or made obsolete in the process. The employees concerned were, in most cases, transferred to other jobs, often better ones. The need for management personnel, on the other hand, has been actually increased as computers generate valuable action data, which was not previously obtainable, and which requires handling at responsible levels. It is estimated that by 1975, about 27 percent of the nation's work force will be in managerial or semimanagerial positions. A good many of these will be computer-related ones whose functions were not included only a few years ago among the more than 30,000 job descriptions listed in the *Dictionary of Occupational Titles,* the bible of personnel professionals, published by the U.S. Employment Service.

Other predictions of how computers would change the ways in which people work have also failed to materialize. For instance, the general reduction of the white-collar workweek from 40 to 35 hours since the 1950s owes far more to employee mobility than to automation. The once widely anticipated four-day week remains stalled by concerted labor and management opposition and by legislation regarding overtime work. The three-day week, however, is catching on, and in the most appropriate places—computer installations—because it allows expensive equipment to be run by two weekly shifts at maximum productivity and without a Saturday break!

Claims made for the computer's future effects have similarly failed to materialize in most other areas of direct social impact—in law, medicine, public and private administration. In part, this has been because many projects were too ambitious for the existing state of the art and will remain so for a long time. For instance, truly effective computer-aided education, below the college level, is still several years away (the equipment is there, but some of the software and most of the instructional material are lacking—primarily a human failure). Often, however, these setbacks have been caused by the lack of large-needed investments of time, money, and human resources. Yet, investments of nearly equal magnitude have been made in other areas where an immediate dollar or defense returns were foreseen. The banking business for one has immensely expanded the range of its services and increased the speed and efficiency with which it handles traditional tasks. The airlines would also have found it difficult to support their huge expansion since the 1950s if they did not have computerized systems for every task—from reservations to traffic control. There are many other examples, such as in the defense area where our armed forces might prefer to give up much of their weaponry rather than their computers.

Thus, where shall a balance be struck? Should there be a point beyond which development of the computer and its technology for social ends, to aid people as individuals, must be emphasized? An answer would be readily forthcoming if society, having analyzed the relationships of technology and civilization, had scheduled coming events, and their character, degree, and timing. We have no such schedule, but when we come together as individuals to form society, then we have a masterful resource. Ours is the power, which we will have to exercise, to allocate resources and shape policies so as to strike a balance between the use and development of the computer and the pace and nature of the social change that we desire, or that we can endure.

AUTOMATION IN MAN'S IMAGE

One of man's oldest legends has been, in many and varied forms, that of the Sorcerer's Apprentice who came to grief when he could not control the creations of his half-baked magic. This theme seems often to be reflected in the feelings that many of us have about the computer and automation. But, there is little that is new in this, for man has perpetually been developing new technologies to satisfy his needs and then bewailing their unexpected or unwanted side effects.

How unpleasant the effects of technological progress can seem to some is brought out in a statement made in 1926 by John E. Edgerton, president of the National Association of Manufacturers. Advances in automation, or as it was then termed, mechanization, had made possible the institution of a five-day week by Henry Ford, a revolutionary development at the time. Speaking in opposition, Edgerton declared:

> I regard a five-day week as an unworthy ideal. . . . More work and better work is a more inspiring and worthier motto than less work and more pay. . . . It is better not to trifle or tamper with God's laws.[2]

2 Russel R. Dynes et al., *Social Problems: Dissensus and Deviation in an Industrial Society* (New York: New York University Press, 1964), p. 285.

But, alas for Mr. Edgerton, mankind has always felt the effects of its own technology, even when it was careful not to "trifle or tamper" with divine ordinances. This was certainly the case during the Middle Ages, but despite its emphasis on faith, civilization was then squarely based on technological factors. One factor was certainly the furrow-turning moldboard plow brought in by Germanic invaders. This heavy plow, pulled by oxen, first made possible the tilling of the fertile clayey soils of most of northwestern Europe, impractical for the lighter digging sticklike devices of the Mediterranean basin. Until that time, most of England and northern France were uncultivated, covered by dense forests. This, more than anything else, caused the shift in power away from the lands of the former Roman Empire.

Another technological basis of medieval civilization was provided by the stirrup, which enabled an armored rider to stay on his mount, sweeping the field before him, unconquerable save by other armored riders. The adoption of the stirrup from the Ural-Altaic people of Asia thus led to the establishment of feudalism in Europe—with society organized to support a landed aristocracy of mounted knights and to bear the cost of their steeds, armor, and weapons.

The adoption of medieval society's two technological pillars reflected deeply felt needs. The furrow-turning moldboard plow helped satisfy the land hunger of the barbarian Germanic invaders, more farmers than warriors, who themselves were being pushed westward by nomadic raiders from the East. The stirrup made possible the creation of cavalry that could meet these nomads on an equal footing and push them back from civilization. Similarly, new technologies and inventions have been summoned to meet the consciously felt needs of other societies in other times—or at least the needs felt by the men who ruled these societies. The justification for meeting these needs was sometimes questioned. Leonardo da Vinci, for example, deliberately concealed some of his ideas that he felt to be too dangerous, such as that for a submarine, "on account of the evil nature of men who would practice assassination at the bottom of the sea." However, the needed knowledge was eventually found, despite all conceivable obstacles. The Quaker faith of the 18th-century mathematician Benjamin Robbins did not prevent him from turning his skills to ballistic calculations for the greater glory of British artillery.

The fortuitous way in which technology is developed in direct response to immediate human needs has been repeatedly demonstrated by the nearly simultaneous development of the same inventions by different men in different countries. In the case of the computer, for instance, while credit for the invention clearly belongs to Eckert and Mauchly, some of the credit for subsequent early developments can be claimed by the University of Birmingham in England and Machines Bull in France. Simultaneous (or nearly so) discovery even occurs for the facile names that catch the fancy of the press and, after wide exposure, become standard terms. Thus, several men have claimed credit for coining the term *automation*. This recognition probably belongs to Delmar S. Harder, former vice-president and director of manufacturing at the Ford Motor Company. He is supposed to have invented the term in 1946 at a conference at which his engineers were describing the latest types of automatic machinery to be installed in a new plant. No longer containing his growing enthusiasm, Harder at last exclaimed "Give us more of that automatic business . . . some more of that—that *automation!*"

The readiness with which man has continuously brought forth new inventions and new technologies is supported by his steady development of better tools. In one of his works, *Sartor Resartus* (1833), Thomas Carlyle wrote: "Man is a tool-using animal. Weak in himself . . . nevertheless he can use tools, can devise tools. . . . Nowhere do you find him without tools; without tools he is nothing, with tools he is all." But as Benjamin Franklin earlier recognized, man is not merely a tool-using animal, he is a toolmaking one—and it should be underscored, one who is dependent upon tools for his continued existence.

However, simply having tools and using them are not enough. What makes man unique as a tool-user and as a toolmaker is the complexity and quality of his tools. The most important feature of these tools is not so much the materials that have been transformed into tools, and the tools with which to make further tools, but the organization of ideas that enable man to transform and to some extent control, not only the world as he finds it, but also the world as he remakes it. *Homo faber*, man the maker, not only makes things, he also makes himself. Man is, indeed, the most remarkable of all his creations. He owes his creativeness almost entirely to his being both a creator and a creature of ideas, a creature who manipulates the environment to suit his own purposes, through the instrumentality of ideas, concepts, mental·images, and abstractions—in short, with symbols. He is the symbol-making and symbol-using animal.

Man creates his own environments through his capacity for abstraction. The man-made part of the environment, that is to say, the learned part, is culture, man's pots and pans, his institutions, and his customs—the information of the past working on the present to modify and control the future. It is his ability to intellectualize physical experience, and communicate successfully certain forms of behavior, to make the most appropriately successful response—not reaction—to the particular challenge of the situation, that distinguishes man from all other creatures. Man is the complex, tool-making animal because he can process information abstractly. Thus his symbols are his most important tools. Symbols are created in the mind or conceptualized; they have no counterpart in the external world. Nevertheless, the human animal learns not only to create them, but to project them upon the external world, and there transform them into reality—Man the symbol-maker, *Homo symbolicus.*

In the course of his cultural evolution, man has become increasingly complex, and so have his symbols. The information-processing capability of *Homo symbolicus* must thus necessarily be at a level of complexity that exceeds anything that has hitherto been known. It is, therefore, hardly surprising that man, without even setting out to do so, developed a means of expanding his information-processing capabilities by building the computer. The computer, after all, serves chiefly to handle the symbols created by man and to elaborate them. We can thus see from this that automation has been developed not alone as a reflection of man's needs but also as a consequence of his changing self-image.

THE REASONS WHY

A widely repeated statement concerning the spread of technology is that 90 percent of all scientists who ever lived are alive and working today. This is easy to believe, considering the rate at which new products and technological achievements keep being announced. However, is this so important? One of those who thinks that it may not be is, surprisingly, one of automation's statesmen, Gordon Smith, a veteran spokesman for the computer community, who has served as executive director of the Association for Computing Machinery, the community's professional society.

It would be much more to the point, Smith states, to stress that 90 percent—and more—of all managers who ever lived are alive and working today, and the impact of their contributions to modern management methods is just beginning to be felt. Automation, he believes, is just one aspect of a cultural and social and, therefore, essentially human upheaval. Modern management methods, likewise, are essentially concerned with human relationships and aspirations. Without computers, these methods would be difficult to implement, but then, without these methods the role of the computer would be much reduced. Both of these developments reflect related human needs, and this—there is no other reason—is why they were developed.

It must be stressed that the development of the computer was in response to the requirements of society. Otherwise, it becomes too easy to forget that it is a tool and, viewing its power, to see it as a danger—as in the case of Erich Fromm, who, in his book *The Sane Society*, writes: "The danger of the past was that men became slaves. The danger of the future is that men may become robots." But the emotional perils run both ways, and excessive fear of the computer may be replaced by excessive glorification of the machine. Thus, the computer specialist's classic GIGO—"Garbage In Garbage Out"—is all too often replaced by another GIGO—"Garbage In, Gospel Out."

It is important that we strike a course between both extremes of feelings concerning the computer—to see it as a useful tool that we must plan to use wisely and well. Otherwise, whichever side we err on, we face, Gordon Smith warns, an ever-present danger. This is a negative phenomenon that represents the other side of the coin of technological progress. It accounts for much of the bewilderment, frustration, and disorientation that accompanies many of what would otherwise be our proudest achievements—and it is called *technological backlash*.

Technological backlash simply means that for every step forward—for every new technological innovation—we often take a step backward as new and unforeseen problems develop. The meaning seems simple, but its effects, in practice, are incredibly complex. An analogy is perhaps provided by the story of the man with a badly infected leg who was told by his doctor that gangrene had developed and the leg would have to be promptly amputated. When after the operation, the patient came out of anesthesia, the doctor came to him and said, "I have good news and bad news—first, the bad news—we amputated the wrong leg—but, now for the good news, your bad leg is getting better!"

TECHNOLOGICAL DEVELOPMENT—
STRAIGHTENING THE COURSE

In previous pages we have said that a new technology, such as that of the computer, will be created when society desires it badly enough. This belief is certainly supported by the results of the survey of public attitudes—with 89 percent of those interviewed feeling that many of the things that we do today would be impossible without computers, and 60 percent believing that American business would now be in serious trouble without computers. These feelings are as new as they are widespread, and this highlights one of the factors that has been a major constraint on technological development—that, before it is developed, not only must a new technology be needed, but the need for it must be widely acknowledged.

One of the wonders about the computer may not be that it is with us, but rather that it was not invented sooner. Electronic models were certainly not practical until 1946. However, electromechanical, or even wholly mechanical models providing quite acceptable performance could well have been developed prior to Aiken's Automatic Sequence Controlled Calculator, conceived in 1937 and only completed in 1944. We might, for instance, wonder (while being thankful for it) why Nazi Germany, which has been the birthplace and home of many of the world's leading mathematicians, did not develop such a device, which was wholly within the state of the art of the late 1930s in Europe. It would probably have speeded the development of the V series rocket weapons. Would the Normandy landings then have been possible with invasion fleets decimated by V2 bombardments? Nor can we doubt that Eichmann and others of the concentration camps' grim bureaucracy would have welcomed the computer's efficiency. In this country, on the other hand, it was the navy's wartime support that hastened the development of Aiken's machine.

Going much further back, we come to Charles Babbage, who in the first half of the 19th century attempted to build his Difference Engine, the first true computer. It is claimed that the technology of the time was not up to building the mechanical device, but the major stumbling block may well have been the sheer scale of Babbage's scheme. His machine would have been more powerful than the first electronic computers. One cannot but wonder what might have occurred if he had been content to introduce a smaller device in the

1830s, which would probably have been speedily improved on as it came into wider use. Perhaps, lapsing into science fiction, there might by 1863 have been a steam-driven Difference Engine clicking away at the Virginia Military Institute and, on-line through a land telegraph line, helping to plot the strategy of the Battle of Gettysburg. Conceivably, Pickett's fateful charge might have been averted, and who knows under what circumstances the Stars and Bars might not be flying today?

Obviously, there was a need for computers then as now, but, the need not being widely realized, the technology was not developed—and this is where and how conditions today differ from those of the past. The development of needed technologies is no longer dependent upon a popularity poll. Instead, their desirability can be considered and the actual development planned and scheduled by a select committee of expert technocrats. The overall progress of technology is itself responsible for this condition. We must no longer, as in the past, base future planning on the capabilities of present technology. Instead, we can count on its steady advance so that we can decide what we want to accomplish, when and how.

How new the current situation is can be indicated by the fact that when in 1945 the United States exploded the first atomic bomb, there was no clear assurance that the device would actually detonate—and that if it did so, the result would not be a firecracker pop, or a world-sweeping chain reaction. By contrast, the feasibility of the NASA moon shots, a project of even greater physical and scientific magnitude, was never in doubt. What slippage has occurred has been due to budgetary stretch-outs or to routine engineering problems—not to fundamental technological defects.

This state of affairs is not quite as splendid as it might seem—for it presents us as individuals, and society as a whole, with a seemingly unending series of decisions concerning the technological achievements that we will need and want in the future. These are cruel choices, for, as we know from previous experiences, there is no way in which a new technology can come about without creating an often unpredictable backlash. Thus, we are faced constantly with a succession of tradeoffs. Each is a painful one to resolve—perhaps giving some ground to the bitter comment of Marcel Pagnol, the French playwright, that "one has to look out for engineers. They begin with sewing-machines, and end up with the atomic bomb."

COMPLEXITY AND CHANGE

Pagnol's feelings appear to be shared by many people who may admire the computer's powers but fear its effects. Thus, of those interviewed in the attitude survey, 55 percent felt that people are becoming too dependent on the computer, and 54 percent believed that it was dehumanizing people and turning them into numbers. Going further afield, 33 percent thought that computers will decrease our freedoms, while 23 percent, nearly one quarter of all those interviewed, feared that computers of the future might disobey the instructions of those who run them.

There is little ground for fearing a computer rebellion, but there is much more reason for fearing an anticomputer ground swell. The danger is not one of machine smashing. That has happened time and again in history. During the Luddite disturbances, for instance, between 1811 and 1816, British workmen smashed new production equipment that was blamed for unemployment and low wages. Machines are easily replaced. The true danger is that men, out of their uncertainties, fears, and doubts, will close their minds to how the computer can be used for their future good.

Automation has been blamed for many of the stresses—human depersonalization, feelings of helplessness—to which individuals are subjected in an industrial society. These, however, did not originate with the computer, but with the steadily greater centralization of power brought about by the Industrial Revolution. Rigid organizational structures, allowing little room for individual action, were needed to create and maintain vast enterprises at a time when the means for controlling complex processes and channeling information were very crude. With the computer, these means are no longer crude, and the need for the rigid structures of the past is increasingly in doubt. The very efficiency with which computers can bring detailed and precise information to central management also makes it possible for the same organizations to enjoy the benefits and flexibility of decentralization.

Centralization, however, is not always a bad thing, and the computer will certainly be a factor in helping reduce through consolidation the gross inefficiencies of many lower-level government units—caused by their excessive numbers and overlaps. At the start of the 1970s, there were in the United States 50 states, 3,043 counties, 17,144 towns and townships, 17,997 municipalities, 34,678 school districts, and 18,323 special districts—together, 91,236 political areas; the number of their individual bureaus, departments, agencies, and other internal bodies was impossible to estimate.

The computer is the agent of change, and change means complexity, as old certainties disappear and new speculations crowd in to be considered. For instance, we have said before that the computer has not reduced total employment. It has increased it if anything. A report of the International Labor Organization, published in 1967, stated that a 1959 ILO report had been wrong in concluding that automation in offices would reduce opportunities for employee promotions. Promotions were certainly plentiful in the 1960s, when a labor shortage was combined with an economic boom. However, this was accompanied by the attrition or early retirement of many older employees in obsolete jobs and the elimination of some middle management positions (the latter both concealed by the economic expansion of the period and revealed by reorganizations following mergers). Nowadays, with the boom deflated and with even computer specialists finding employment more difficult to come by, there is no more slack. The impact of the computer on the size and nature of office employment may well receive a second test.

We could well also wonder whether the computer will influence other aspects of our daily lives and work. Thus, there is the problem of leisure, which we seem to have less and less of. It was not always so. During nearly one-third (109 days) of the ancient Roman 355-day calendar, fiscal or judicial business could not be legally transacted. The number of Roman holidays peaked in the middle of the fourth century when it reached 175 days. In the early 19th century, French intellectuals worked an average of 2,500 hours per year.[3] By 1950, they were working 3,000 to 3,500 hours annually. Today, as we know, the leisure class is not composed of the leaders of our society and economy. These leaders are the ones who work hardest and longest. For them, status and leisure are in an inverse ratio. Much of their time is not spent in actually making decisions or performing significant tasks. Instead, they must devote long hours to the examination of extensive, detailed, and often scattered information. The gathering of these data and its editing into a concise format is one of the tasks for

---

3 Harold L. Wilensky, "Uneven Distribution of Leisure: The Impact of Economic Growth on Free Time ," *Social Problems*, Summer 1964, pp. 33-35.

which computers can be used most effectively. The computers may thus, in time, serve to redress the balance of leisure for their users.

The computer is distinguished today by its enormous complexity. This complexity appears in its use, which is limited to a relatively small number of professionals, in the vast potential for errors that exists, and in the unexpected consequences that may arise from its proper use. This complexity, however, is not innate to the technology but, rather, exists because the computer is still a relatively recent invention, not having come into widespread use until the early to mid-1960s.

We are reminded by Gordon Smith that the advance of a technology does tend to ease some of the problems brought about by its early complexity. At one time, he points out, it took real knowledge and quite a bit of equipment to take good pictures with one of the early cameras. Today, most modern cameras do everything automatically. Similarly, 98 percent of all automobiles now have automatic shifts, but most drivers do not understand the internal combustion engine. All they need to know is how to drive well enough so that they will not kill others, if not themselves. Smith feels that computer automation will undergo the same evolution and will become ever easier to use by unsophisticated users.

We may derive only partial comfort from the computer becoming a tool that we can use and control directly—for then we will be compelled to take an active role in the socioeconomic revolution that we are living in. When the pace of change, the rate of evolution, becomes too rapid, the result is no longer evolution but revolution. This current revolution may be the most disturbing upheaval yet to occur. It is easy to bow to superior strength or to tyranny, no matter with how many inward protests. But how much harder it is to do what we must do—to accept an infinity of choices—a situation where all the "Verboten" and "Stop" signs are gone and the safety handrails have been taken away. Such is the age of automation. This is the age of the computer—when there are so many choices to be made, and all those choices are up to us. These choices are difficult ones, and they represent heavy burdens, but perhaps the heaviest burdens we bear are those we refuse to take up.

2

Revolution and Evolution

Revolution and evolution are but two descriptions of the same process of growth and change. They differ only in the time frame that each involves, but it is an enormous difference—or is it? Nothing may seem slower to us than the five million years and more during which an apelike biped shambled through prehistory on his way to becoming man. But, gauged by another time scale, the measured span of man's evolution blurs like a speeded-up film frame into a revolution—the revolt of an entire species against the order of nature as it had, hitherto, always been.

The creation of man is a revolutionary event, because it is a self-made, a conscious one. The proudest creation of *Homo faber,* man the maker, is himself. He owes his creativeness, his ability to manipulate the environment around him, to the fact that he is both a creator and a manipulator of ideas, the symbol-using animal.

The degree to which his intellectualizing, his reliance on symbols, has differentiated man from other creatures is demonstrated by his well-documented lack of instinctive animal reactions. These were lost many hundreds of thousands of years ago. Today, both men and apes share a common inability to make some vital responses instinc-

17

tively. They can, for instance, neither nurse their babies nor copulate[1] without instruction. With these instinctive abilities lost, man has had no choice but to go forward, if only for survival. And go forward he has, for the power to use symbols, which distinguishes man, has been made possible by the steady growth of his physical ability to foster and develop these powers. The human brain now contains, on the average, up to 13 billion neurons, nerve cells which have up to 25,000 possible connections with other neurons. By contrast, the brain of the man-like australopithecine of over two million years ago held no more than 5.5 billion neurons, and that of the Peking man, less than a million years old, still boasted fewer than 9.4 billion. Thus, in less than three million years, the size and complexity of the brain has nearly tripled, representing a gigantic change that must have affected every gene in the human body.

Considering the way that he has remade himself, *Homo faber* can truly boast that he is his own most remarkable creation. He is the end product of millennia of mutations and selective breeding, and his genes are generally those of the strongest and smartest men of the species, if only because, until recently, men who were both weak and stupid seldom lived long enough to pass on their deficiencies. These genes are also those of the most powerful men who, through their strength and status, probably through more than one woman, transmitted their genetic traits.

Some men enjoyed more success than others. In more recent times, some of these successes seemed to have hypertrophied. In the 19th century, for example, King Mtessa of Uganda had 7,000 wives. Victorian explorers computed with some awe that even if he cohabited with each wife only once a year, he would still have been confronted with 19 spouses a day. Whatever his success may have been in fulfilling this goal, it is certain that Mtessa's descendants are numerous in Uganda.

TECHNOLOGY'S MANY REVOLUTIONS

Man has constantly re-created himself—not into his image, as he was in the past, but into that of an improved, more capable version

---

[1] Men and apes share with many other animals their inability to mate instinctively. For example, when a pair of pandas were to be sent to the United States, following President Nixon's visit to China, the young animals were first kept at the Peking Zoo to watch older pandas and learn from them.

of himself. As a function of this re-creation—to improve his security and well-being—man has also changed the world around him through the development of new technologies in increasingly rapid succession. As each of these technologies has been developed and put to use, the effects on man and his environment have been striking and startlingly swift and, each time, mankind has had to struggle and live through a difficult period of transition.

We are living today in just such a period of transition—that caused by the sudden appearance of the computer, which has begun to play a major role in our society and in our lives. Whatever happens, we are going to have to live with the computer. It is here to stay. This coexistence can be for us one filled with fear or distaste, or it can be a constructive partnership in which we are alert for ways through which we can benefit from the machine's capabilities. We can achieve this partnership more easily if we abandon our awe of the computer and if we see it in perspective—as but the latest of a long succession of major technological developments that rival it in importance.

Probably the best way in which we can gain this perspective is to stop thinking of the Industrial Revolution of the 18th century as man's first major technological revolution. There are at least seven of these upheavals that have occurred in the history of man's social development—from the shaping of the first hand ax to, and including, the computer:

1. The discovery and development of toolmaking
2. The emergence of hunting as a way of life
3. The discovery and use of fire
4. The emergence of agriculture and pastoralism
5. The development of cities and an urban civilization
6. The 18th-century industrial revolution and the birth of modern technology
7. The development of the computer, which may in time support the addition of an eighth item to this list.[2]

The examination of each of these revolutions and the fundamental effects they have had on mankind and its development may

2 Since the control of human population growth is ultimately likely to be solved by the "pill," its invention should certainly be added to these major technological revolutions.

help us place the computer revolution in its true perspective. It may also show us that if the impact of computers is but a fraction of that generated by earlier technologies, then this revolution will be of awesome magnitude.

TOOLMAKING

When a man-like ape began making and using tools upon which he then depended for his continued survival, he became man. Essentially, a tool is an object that enables its user to extend the power of both his mind and his body. As we have noted, Benjamin Franklin first defined man as a tool-making animal. It was a good definition, but not quite complete. Our nearest relatives, gorillas, chimpanzees, and orangutans, are all capable of making simple tools. Also, there are a number of other animals who habitually use tools, although they do not make them. The burrowing wasp *Ammophila* uses a small pebble as a hammer to pound down the soil over its nest of eggs. One of Darwin's finches of the Galápagos islands, *Cactospiza*, secures a cactus spine in its beak to pick insects from the crevices in the bark of trees. The British greater spotted woodpecker uses clefts in tree trunks as vises into which it pushes pine cones so that they are firmly held while it pulls out the seeds. The southern and Californian sea otters use a stone, which they carry with them in the water, as both a hammer and an anvil for breaking the hard shells of the shellfish they eat. The Australian Arnhem Land firehawk, or kitehawk, picks up smoldering sticks in its claws and drops them into dry patches of grass and then waits with its companions for the exodus of frightened animals attempting to escape the fire, and falls upon them as they flee. Egyptian vultures pick up stones in their beaks and throw them at ostrich eggs to break the shells and feast on the contents.

These are not instinctive forms of behavior—that is, they were not innately inherited—but socially learned. In these animals, such elementary forms of tool using constitute inventions that significantly contributed to their survival. However, none of these animals, and, indeed, no animal other than man depends on tools for its continued existence.

Man is unique among all creatures, not only because of the quality and complexity of his tools but also because of the ideas that he generates and the symbols he uses in order to create these tools.

This ability to process information abstractly enables man to make an appropriate response—not just a reaction—to a particular challenge in a specific situation. Symbols are the most important tools of *Homo symbolicus,* man the symbolmaker.

A symbol, as used here, is an abstraction or organization of ideas that represent something having no external reality outside the mind. Experienced mentally, symbols constitute no part of the external world, but nevertheless remain essentially part of the human world. Symbols have functional value only. Signals differ from symbols in that the meanings they convey are derived from the physical form they take in the external world. Most communication between animals is of the signaling variety, through obvious changes in behavior known as "mood convection." Man alone communicates virtually exclusively through symbols.

Many animals are capable of some symbol usage, and there can be little doubt that man's protohuman ancestors used symbols long before any of them made a complex physical tool. The contemporary great apes use symbols to a limited degree, and, under challenging conditions, sometimes exhibit quite remarkable innovatory behavior. For example, a chimpanzee will place box upon box and then climb the structure to reach a bunch of bananas. This ape will also insert one stick into another to make a pole for reaching bananas. Chimpanzees and orangutans will fold straw into a firm implement to reach desired objects. Under natural conditions, chimpanzees have been observed to pick a straw or dried grass stem and poke it carefully down a hole in a termite heap. The termites attempting to defend their heap bite the straw and cling to it; the chimpanzee, familiar with their behavior, gently withdraws the stem, and, licking off the adhering termites, munches them with relish. Dr. Jane Goodall has seen chimpanzees actually prepare for the event by breaking off a twig from a tree, stripping it of leaves and side-stems, and going from one termite hill to another, sedulously searching for a meal.

If a tool is an object modified or changed to act upon something else, then quite clearly the chimpanzee and orangutan are not only rudimentary toolmakers, but capable of conceptualizing the making and use of a simple tool for an immediate future purpose. One of the authors (Ashley Montagu) has seen an orangutan in a cage at the Bronx Zoo in New York pick up the straw from the floor and clumping it together make a firm pole of it to reach an otherwise unattainable object. Under natural conditions, the gorilla lives in so rich a food area that it appears to have no incentive for making tools. However, there can be little doubt that he can make simple ones when sufficiently motivated.

As might be expected, there is a continuation of the rudimentary tool-modifying activity of the ape and the toolmaking of the earliest men. The difference between the toolmaking of apes and man lies in the increase in the complexity of man's tools. However, it may be well to remember that this difference in complexity has not been truly significant during most of man's five million or so years of existence as a recognizable separate genus. True, man had developed many tools that could help him to better clothe, feed, and defend himself. However, while they had helped, none had fully revolutionized his life. This came about only 8,000 or 9,000 years ago, sometime before 6000 B.C., with the invention of the hafted-ax.

Man had long used hand axes, which could be very sharp indeed, but were of limited usefulness. The hafted ax was a successful modification of these hand axes that could be used to chop down trees and clear away underbrush, as well as a hunting weapon and a tool with which to cut or scrape leather and pelts. Shaped like a modern though thicker ax head, it originally lacked a handle and was grasped at its blunt end with one hand. This was a crude tool, but infinitely superior to any that had existed before. The theory, at least, of agriculture had just then been discovered by Neolithic man, but it is unlikely that this theory could have been put into practice and extended in many places if man had not at least possessed a tool that would enable him to cut clearing from the forest in which to grow his first meager crops.

It is estimated that the world's population numbered no more than 10 million at the time that the hafted-ax was invented. It is also thought that this number would have increased only slowly, if at all, if the tool had not become available to make agriculture possible. In fact, there has been speculation that if the hafted-ax had not been invented, the entire development of our modern civilization would never have taken place, and we would still be living much as did our Stone Age ancestors, with little advantage over apes through our physical tools.

After the hafted-ax came into wide use, the pace of human development became ever faster, and, with it, human history began. Little more than 4,000 or 5,000 years later, we find the Egyptians of 4000 B.C. transporting stones averaging 2.5 tons apiece to build the

Great Pyramid. They had no pulleys. These did not come until about 300 B.C. They were thus limited to sleds (their runners lubricated with milk), rollers, ropes, and lots of manpower. These were crude tools, but they were certainly far more powerful and sophisticated, compared with those that existed at the time the hafted-ax was invented, than ours are today, compared with those of the ancient Egyptians.

From 4000 B.C. onward, new developments ensued with increasing frequency. The Egyptian sleds gave way by 3500 B.C. to the first wheeled carts developed in Mesopotamia. Then came the use of horses and camels to carry loads in about 2000 B.C. At the beginning of the Christian era, the first water mills were built in the Mediterranean basin. By A.D. 300, the Chinese had finally developed a collar that enabled horses to pull heavy loads without being choked. The collar took 600 years to travel to Europe, which, one century later, in A.D. 1000, took up the windmill, first used in Persia in A.D. 600.

Yet, until A.D. 1500, the pace of man's toolmaking technology advanced only slowly and fitfully. It was only then that this pace began to accelerate steadily, becoming more rapid with each succeeding generation. With its advance came the new means of power that were to change man's world in 200 years in a manner unlike anything that had previously occurred in all the millions of years of man's development. First, there was the steam engine, invented and reinvented throughout Western Europe, but finally becoming firmly established in England at the end of the 1700s. Then, in the 1890s, the development of practical internal combustion engines. As we know, there have since then been other developments, including the unleashing of the atom in the early 1940s, and, not long afterwards, in the same decade, the creation of the computer.

There has thus been a steady and manifest increase in the complexity of man's tools during the course of his history. These increases have reflected the correspondingly greater complexity of man's ideas. The result of this combination of both physical and intellectual complexities has been the occurrence of major social upheavals that have also been technological revolutions.

HUNTING AS A WAY OF LIFE

All members of the order Primates, except man and a few monkeys, are forest dwellers, and all of them, except man, are predominantly vegetarian. Forest dwellers are abundantly supplied with all the plant foods they need. Their table is, as it were, laid, and all they have to do is eat.

Fairly recently as geologic periods run, during the Pliocene, which ended a scant two million years ago, changes in the climate resulted in the deforestation of large parts of Africa south of the equator, leaving man's progenitors out on the open savannas where the vegetation was insufficient to maintain life. They responded to this challenge at first by using for food all the small and slow-moving animals they could gather. Then, they set out deliberately to hunt all other beasts. They had, in effect, developed hunting as a formal and deliberate way of life.

The development of toolmaking possibly either parallels or was given a strong impetus by the development of hunting, for hunters needed more and better tools with which to kill their prey and then cut the meat and scrape its pelt. These were forthcoming, and the primitive hunter's flint-tipped spear could be hurled with fair accuracy as far as 150 feet. Then, between 30,000 and 15,000 B.C., came the invention of the bow and arrow, possibly in North Africa. It was a remarkable tool, not merely because of its power, but because it was a wholly abstract creation. Unlike the spear, for instance, it was not an extension of the human arm, but a device whose creation was based entirely on the application of physical principles. The bow itself was soon rivaled by another creation of primitive technology, the slot and javelin, used to cast a small spear farther than a human arm could hurl it. During his explorations of the South Pacific in the 18th century, Captain James Cook found the device to be deadlier and more accurate at up to 150 feet than his own muskets.

Hunting was perhaps the most important of all the inventions that led to the development of modern man, for it placed a very high premium upon the development of problem-solving abilities. Hunters on the open savanna were faced with an enormous number of challenging situations requiring quick and appropriate responses, and it was those who responded best who survived to pass on their genes and, through natural selection, foster the development of the intelligence that distinguishes man from all other creatures.

Among the talents that were passed on by successful hunters, one of the most important may have been that of conscious language. Until then, man had had little need for one. Even toolmaking required little skill at communication. In hunting, however, two types of communications were required—to plan the hunt ahead of time and to exchange information and instructions during its course. This probably became even more important during the glacial periods when man survived through cooperative hunting of big game—mammoth, bison, eland. Another contribution of hunting to the human race, a nongenetic one this time, may have been the dog, a creature similar to the wolf, though with smaller jaws, which became man's companion around 10,000 B.C. The dog's hunting role is, however, disputed by some who trace its ancestry closer to the jackal and claim that, initially, its chief role in the human community was that of a scavenger.

The evolution of man spans approximately five and a half million years, and during nearly all of that time man has been a hunter. There are still a number of people among us today who have never known any other way of life. These are the remnants of the Australian aborigines, the Bushmen of the Kalahari Desert, the Pygmies of the Ituri Forest in the Congo, the Eskimo, and the Semai of Malaya.

Hunting began by making human life possible. But, in the long run, it provided a base for the many other developments that have fostered the unique human behavioral potentialities that characterize man.

THE DISCOVERY OF FIRE

The earliest known use of fire by man occurred some 750,000 years ago in the Escale cave of southeastern France. The use of fire and the making of fire are, of course, two different things, the use being undoubtedly much older. Several contemporary people, the Pygmies of the Ituri Forest and the pygmy Andaman Islanders, use but still do not make fire. Firemaking by man at Chou-kou-tien in China about 300,000 years ago was apparently for warmth only, as there is no evidence that fire was used for either cooking or the shaping and hardening of wooden implements until thousands of years afterwards.

The use of fire was an important technological advance for man, but the ability to make it was even more important. It greatly expanded his ability to keep himself warm, cook food, harden pointed sticks and spears, clear ground of undesired brush, and heat water. Also, of course, fire provided light and so increased the length of the day that man's routine was no longer dependent on the sun. He could sit with his family and companions into the night and talk, reminisce, and plan. The fireside became an intrinsic part of daily life; it became an institution. The older people could, in the pleasant glow of a comfortable fire, transmit informally much of their society's knowledge and wisdom. In this way, fire served to bring the members of the group more closely together. With firelight, prehistoric man was able to explore the depths and otherwise inaccessible recesses of caves, and to use them as sanctuaries and places of worship, his own home being at the mouth of the cave.

Thus, the use of fire has produced revolutionary social changes whose impact continues.

AGRICULTURE AND PASTORALISM

It is generally believed that agriculture, the control of the reproduction of plants, was initiated by women. Women have in all cultures been the food gatherers, while men have been the more active hunters. In regions in which the soil was particularly fertile, and seasonal flooding occurred (for example, in the region between the Euphrates and the Tigris rivers in Mesopotamia), women probably observed that seeds dropped from plants they gathered germinated and grew into full plants. An obvious next step was the deliberate sowing of seeds and the subsequent harvesting of the fully grown plants. The Neolithic ladies did their work so well that the domestication of nearly all of our present-day cultivated plants had begun well before the Bronze Age. Two of the basic species, in fact, wheat and barley, are known only in association with man. Among many societies, the sowing of seeds and harvesting are still woman's occupation.

By 7000 B.C., agriculture was well established in Jordan, Iran, and Anatolia, and man was living in permanent settlements. Remains of cemeteries and graves containing luxury objects indicate that man now enjoyed leisure and time to occupy himself with other things than appeasing his hunger. The domestication of animals undoubtedly preceded the discovery of agriculture, for the first domesticated sheep are found in the Middle East as early as 7500 B.C. Agriculture made it possible to enlarge the range of animals that could be domesticated and fed from supplies of stored feed.

Agriculture included highly organized cooperative community activities such as the building of permanent facilities in which to store harvests, and enclosures for domestic animals. Records of all deliveries and withdrawals of stored food and fodder had to be kept and carefully supervised and regulated. Social organization became increasingly ordered, and people became more closely knit and disciplined through these procedures—particularly when a high degree of cooperation involving large populations was involved. As long ago as 3000 B.C., most of the population of Egypt was engaged in irrigating the land by dipping water by hand from a well or spring into an irrigation ditch.

At about the same time that the Egyptians were irrigating their land, onagers (wild donkeys) were being used for the first time to pull Sumerian war chariots. True horses appeared in the Middle East from Central Asia 1000 years later, around 2000 B.C. The mobility of horses quickened the pace of history. It promoted warfare and invasions, but it also made possible to an unparalleled degree the exchange of knowledge and of genes between the far-flung outposts of humanity.

Art first appeared in the form of animal carvings and statuettes of the supreme deity, the Mother Goddess. Trading increased, and there is some evidence of raiding. By the end of this period, the Proto-Neolithic, extending from 9000 to 7000 B.C., the first towns came into being, often surrounded by massive defensive walls. During this period, the Fall of Man begins, the decline of man from a cooperative food-gathering hunter living in small groups, to a disoperative 150-pound nonlinear servomechanism that can be wholly reproduced by unskilled labor. Agriculture enabled man to stay in one place, instead of wandering about from place to place in search of food, because now he could control the reproduction of his plants and animals. He need no longer be a food gatherer and hunter, for he could now grow his own plant food and meat supply. Now, also, he could feed many more mouths than formerly, for a food-gathering, hunting population can support only a very small number of people. And so, man began to increase, to multiply, and replenish and subdue the earth . . . with consequences that have been a mixed blessing of abounding miracles and accelerating disasters.

URBANISM AND CIVILIZATION

The emergence of urbanism and the development of civilization go hand in hand. Urbanism came about as a consequence of the demands and responses of an ever-enlarging society that applied its skills and technologies to the more efficient living together of men in increasingly larger communities. Essentially, a civilization results from increasingly complex tools invented in response to the concepts of community life emerging in men's minds.

The first town known to us is Jericho, not the biblical Jericho, but a much older town buried beneath the Jericho of the Bible. This Jericho as a town dates back to 6968 B.C., its beginning going back to the 8th millennium B.C. The town was well fortified, indicating the presence of a strong enemy nearby. Pottery was still unknown in this city, but a fine bone industry flourished. Houses were constructed of long cigar-shaped bricks, with walls and floors carefully plastered. Here, fine limestone plates and bowls first appeared, as did querns (hand mills for grinding grain), opening on one narrow side. Jericho also contained shrines with fertility figures and larger statuary, together with collections of skulls upon which the facial features had been delicately and expertly molded. The houses were quite elaborate, with hearths and courtyards, through the latter of which, in lieu of streets, all communication occurred. The economy remained based on agriculture.

The conditions necessary for the development of civilization are (1) a complex social hierarchy, either royal or theocratic, (2) systematic urbanization, and (3) strong political control and adequate concentration of economic resources.

These conditions do not appear to have occurred together until the later centuries of the 4th millennium B.C., and then only in Sumer and Egypt. But wherever these conditions later arose in China, India, Greece, or Middle America, civilization followed. And with the start of civilization frequently came the adoption of one or a limited number of common languages to replace the multitude of dialects that previously divided men among themselves. The inhabitants of modern New Guinea, who are still mainly at the Neolithic level of civilization, speak approximately 700 mutually unintelligible languages.

Civilization also brought about the development of one of man's most remarkable tools—writing. About 5500 years old, this development required the presence of a strong sense of public and private property. Religious and secular literature could be preserved and transmitted by oral tradition, but commercial transactions, especially when they were conducted on an impersonal level, required a more dependable record than the human memory.

Unquestionably writing was the most important technical invention of the "urban-civilized" society, because human speech could now be recorded in permanent form through a set of conventional symbols. Writing, like most inventions, came about in response to a particular need. With the development of towns and the growth of commerce, transactions were no longer on the simple level of barter between individuals. Instead, they were coming under the supervision of the bureaucracy that, centered on the temples, was beginning to develop, becoming increasingly impersonal, pervasive, and permanent. This was no late development. The first document or inscription indicating the existence of a bureaucracy is from Egypt's Pyramid Age and dates back to about 2400 B.C.—and it is believed that this bureaucracy might already have existed three dynasties before!

There was a pressing need to record the receipt of temple dues, to facilitate commercial transactions, and to keep records of those engaged in sharp practices. Another early use of writing was the recording of the warfare that developed as city vied against city—as in the Stele of the Vultures from early Mesopotamia, which records the victory of King Eannatum of the city of Lagash over the neighboring city of Umma. The cities had at most 35,000 and 16,000 inhabitants respectively.

The fledgling civilized cities and states did not war solely among each other. They also fought fiercely to defend themselves against the nomads and barbarians forever prowling along the frontiers of civilization, always ready to raid and devastate. The most conspicuous of their reactions is certainly the Great Wall of China, erected against the Huns about 200 B.C. The wall did more, however, than simply turn back the Huns. It was a gigantic social breakwater, redirecting the waves of barbarian migration, with the result that the Huns invaded Europe and India because they could not invade China—and their actual invasion was preceded by those of the many peoples and tribes they had set in motion, fleeing before them. The great barbarian invasions that destroyed the Roman Empire of the west in the fifth century A.D. were set off by China's defensive action seven centuries before.

With increased numbers of people within the city, for the first time in the history of man, members of the same population could pass on the street or in the courtyard and not know one another. Impersonality became not only a matter of mercantile transactions but also of the relationship existing among most of the members of their own society. Men with more land than others could grow more crops and domesticate more animals. They could become wealthy and powerful. As Lord Acton has told us, power is something that very few men are able to use wisely. Power, he said, tends to corrupt, and absolute power to corrupt absolutely. Soon there were chieftains who became rulers, a priesthood, masters, foremen, laborers, silver-smiths, scribes, bureaucrats, and a thorough stratification of the classes.

All the basic disorders that plague our modern cities and that have produced the dehumanization of man appeared first in the earliest towns. Complaints of peasants in early Egypt indicate how debasing the effects of urbanism had become. In making himself more comfortable in the world, in reducing the rigors of existence, man became increasingly materialistic and so preoccupied with things that he soon commenced to extend his ideas of power over things to human beings. Human beings became things, tools to serve the pur-poses of others.

The effects of urbanism upon man are evident today. Our large cities constitute the last words in dehumanization, "where wealth accumulates and men decay." Our large cities are no longer manage-able, governable, or livable. Crime, corruption, bankruptcy, ugliness reign supreme. Our cities have failed in what they were originally created to do: bring men together into closer community so that they might reciprocally confer the benefits upon each other that their in-dividual uniquenesses would enable them to contribute. The modern city has failed in the most fundamental objective of all: the humaniz-ing of man.

There were such cities, but they did not long endure. Athens is perhaps the outstanding example of a city-state whose contributions to humanity will endure as long as man exists.

THE 18TH-CENTURY INDUSTRIAL REVOLUTION

Perhaps the first signs of the coming of the 18th-century Indus-trial Revolution occurred about 100 B.C., in the Middle East, when man first used the power of moving water to turn stones for grinding wheat into flour. Several centuries later, in lands without flowing streams, windmills were devised to do the same thing. But it was not until the 14th or 15th century that a great variety of applications for power from water wheels and windmills came about. New machines were invented, especially in England, for sawing wood, crushing ore, pumping forge bellows, raising water from mines, and the like. In the Netherlands, thousands of windmills powered pumps, ground grain, and drove saws.

Although at first, applications of wind power and waterpower did not involve large numbers of people, by the end of the 16th century this began to change. William Lee's invention of a knitting machine that could turn out 10 to 15 times as many stitches as the fastest knitter began to foreshadow the end of handcrafting in the textile industry.

At this point there begin to appear violent human reactions to technical advances. In Danzig in 1596, the inventor of a ribbon loom, which threatened the livelihood of hundreds of artisans, was murdered. Other serious acts of sabotage and violence, both in England and on the continent, expressed the textile workers' fears for their jobs.

During the 18th century, in England, agricultural methods became the object of scientific investigations. A number of improvements were instituted, affecting stock quality and soil treatment. The new methods, combined with increased demands from the European continent, resulted in great increases in acreage under intensive tillage. At about the same time, industry was undergoing great changes, sparked largely by several inventions. In 1770 James Hargreaves patented the spinning jenny. Richard Arkwright invented the water frame in 1771, and in 1779 Samuel Crompton's spinning mule was introduced. These gave impetus to the textile industry. James Watt's patents and successful application of the steam engine to cotton manufacture further increased output.

Other great developments leading to the Industrial Revolution were (1) increased use of iron and steel, (2) invention of more new machines, (3) the factory system, (4) transportation and communications developments, and (5) still greater application of science and technology to industry.

The Industrial Revolution, which in England began about 1750, gave England about a century's head start on her rivals in the competition for world markets. For the next 180 years or more, the lot of the new working classes was pitiful. John and Barbara Hammond have graphically described it in their book, *The Bleak Age* (London, Penguin Books, 1947). For one thing, factories changed man's role in relation to the production process—he either operated a machine or performed routine, relatively unskilled duties. The factory owners' interests dominated the changing relationships. With almost no checks on the profit motive, many harmful practices grew up, and the reactions to these practices eventually had far-reaching consequences. For example, wages were kept at a minimum level, working conditions were abominable, child labor became widespread, safety considerations nearly nonexistent.

The inevitable outcome was the historic series of labor riots and confrontations that began the labor movement. The formation of labor unions and, later, federations of unions, the passage of legislation recognizing bargaining rights of such unions, the prohibition of many vicious practices, the regulation of labor-capital relationships, and above all the recognition at all levels of society of the dignity of the individual worker—these highlight the results of the series of crises brought on by the Industrial Revolution.

With increased power, unions in this country have continued, to some extent, to perpetuate various obstructive or inefficient practices in response to new technology. In the early part of the 20th century, when the window-glass industry began introducing new glassmaking machines, the union of window-glass workers opposed the new methods that were more efficient. Eventually, however, the new processes in that industry displaced the old, and the union was formally disbanded. Union insistence on contract provisions such as rules requiring an enterprise to pay for more hours of work than management considers necessary, or specifying crew size in certain machine operations, or providing for wage differentials for greater skill requirements, have influenced the rate at which technological changes are introduced. And the perpetuation, in some areas, of the practice of featherbedding has caused much public disapproval of union actions. More recently, a variation of featherbedding has appeared in the newspaper and publishing industries, following management proposals to install computer-controlled printing equipment. Because such machines would practically eliminate the linotypers' trades and require extensive retraining efforts to operate new types of machines, the affected unions fought these proposals vigorously. In spite of this opposition, several large newspapers have begun using the new techniques, which offer dramatic increases in efficiency.

Confrontations by representatives of labor and management constitute a complex class of interface in modern society. Although the respective combatting forces have grown more powerful and the consequences of prolonged disputes potentially more damaging than in the past, both sides have profited much from their experiences. Also, public regulating mechanisms have resulted in a better understanding of the causes of economic dislocations. The result is a more favorable climate for seeking solutions through impartial fact finding.

THE COMPUTER

The effects of the computer revolution will be at least as profound as the industrial revolutions that have preceded it. What these effects will be is the subject of extended discussion in other chapters of this book.

In his mechanical-technological age, man himself has increasingly become mechanized and technologized. This is a danger to be avoided. The computer can be misused to make a thing of man. Man must, therefore, always make certain that man remains master of the machine. The computer can become the greatest and most versatile servant man has ever had. Writing was invented to facilitate the accounting of an increasingly complex economy; it subsequently became the vehicle of a highly developed literature. Similarly, the computer, designed to facilitate planning and record keeping for undreamed-of new technologies and a mushrooming worldwide economy, can become the vehicle for the discovery of new and beautiful dimensions of life. The computer can contribute to the fulfillment of every individual and the solution of virtually every human problem. At one time, this was a dream. Man, with a computer, can make it a reality.

3

What the Computer Is

So much is said nowadays about what computers can do that little attention appears to be given to what computers actually are. Yet this is an important question. Computers, like any machine (or biological organism, for that matter), have quite specific limitations as well as potentialities. It would be well for us to understand the nature of the computer if we are to understand its relationship to man.

There are various ways of characterizing computers. Of these, one of the least helpful is the current "in" term, *systems* (a successor to "giant electronic brain," now held in low esteem). *Systems* abound in nature as well as among man's creations. There is, for instance, hardly any system so nearly perfect as that of a beehive or an ant colony. Therefore, the term *system*, when applied to computers, is more generic than descriptive. However, there is a way of describing the computer that would place it in a truer perspective and would be more faithful to the context of this book. This would be to characterize it as man's latest achievement in his never-ending quest for better, more significant, quantification of himself, his fellowmen, and his environment.

Quantification means establishing the quantity or taking the measure of something, or anything. Time, money, volume, weight, area, thoughts, feelings—all these can be measured to varying extents according to various standards. The end product of these measurements is knowledge of (more or less) established reliability. Such knowledge has in the past supported both the survival and the evolution of mankind. This process began immeasurably long ago—with the counting of animals to be hunted or the notching of time periods in sticks or well-polished ivory. When men began to trade among themselves, they had to have some standards with which to measure, to quantify, the value of goods, in respect to the value of other goods. Out of this activity came money, first expressed as a given weight of a specific metal. Agriculture, too, imposed needs for quantification. Ancient Egypt, for instance, lived or starved according to the height of the waters of the Nile. Priest-engineers maintained a system of notched measuring rods through the entire length of the river basin. They used the measurements to forecast the harvest for the year and possible needs for irrigation or damming projects. In a sense, Pharaonic Egypt might be likened to a gigantic analog computer.

PRECOMPUTER DEVELOPMENTS

As his society and economy became steadily more complex, man quickly began to develop and rely on artificial counting aids. The earliest ones were probably simple pebbles piled together to represent numbers. In fact, today's *calculators* owe their name to the Latin word *calculus*, which means pebble. Then, dating from about 450 B.C., came the abacus, which, consisting of beads strung on rods or arranged in grooves, began to be used around the world. The device has been steadily improved and is still in common use throughout

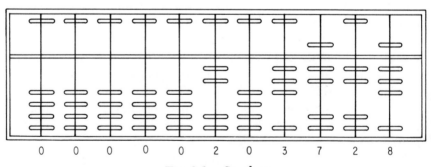

0   0   0   0   0   2   0   3   7   2   8

Fig. 3-1. Soroban

Asia and eastern Europe. One of its most highly developed versions, the Japanese *soroban,* is shown in figure 3-1. The device can be used by a skilled operator to perform all arithmetical calculations as rapidly as with an electromechanical calculator.

In 1642 a teen-age genius named Blaise Pascal invented the first calculator. His calculator could perform addition and subtraction with gears and notched wheels. Designed to help his work in his father's tax collection office in Rouen, France, Pascal's machine had an automatic tens-carrying feature, a breakthrough in the evolution of computing machinery. The same basic method was used by Gottfried Wilhelm von Leibnitz, who, about 1670, developed an improved machine that could also do multiplication and division. Various models of electromechanical calculating devices (including odometers and speedometers) employed today still use notched wheels to represent the decimal digits.

The next important development in digital data representation was the use of holes punched in cards or tape. In 1801 the Frenchman Joseph Marie Jacquard invented an automatic weaving loom which followed instructions punched into cards to weave fabrics of intricate patterns and numerous colors. Though not a calculating device, the Jacquard loom set the stage for the representation of data through holes punched in cards.

The potential of the punched card was first recognized by the 19th-century English philosopher and mathematician, Charles Babbage. Babbage's *Passages from the Life of a Philosopher,* published in 1864, provides a profile of this remarkable man: inventor, creator of a system of mechanical notation, cryptographer, and a founder of several of England's most influential scientific institutions.

In 1822 Babbage proposed the construction of a "Difference Engine," which would both calculate numbers and print the results mechanically to produce mathematical tables. His project received steadily increasing support from the British government, support that totaled about 17,000 pounds, and Babbage spent at least as much of his own money. However, even though his ideas were sound, there were too many obstacles to the successful completion of the machine, not the least being an unending succession of design changes. His machine also would have required about two tons of brass, steel, and pewter clockwork, which in those days would have had to be made to order—and completion of the machine would have probably cost about 50 times as much as he had estimated.

Work on the Difference Engine finally stopped in 1833,[1] but by September of 1834, Babbage had prepared the first drawings of his "Analytical Engine," designed to be "a machine of the most general nature." Although the device had a slow speed of 60 additions per minute, the design embodied all of the basic elements of a digital computer. Two sets of cards were used in its operation: (1) operation cards that contain the series of operations in the order in which they occur, and (2) the variable and constant cards containing the numbers to be acted upon. Holes punched in the cards were sensed by wires spaced to correspond to the card column layout and, when passing through holes, to activate other machine components mechanically. There were several basic units in the design. One, called the "store," was used to store data. Another, the "mill," was to "grind out," or compute, the answers. A third unit, called the "control" was to control the mill's processing of data held in store. In effect, these three units duplicated the functions of a modern computer system.

Babbage's plans called for fulfillment of the following requirements of a "universal analytical tool":

Storing intermediate results for reuse
Punching, display, and printing of output
Error detection and alarm
Conditional alteration of problem direction

To quote Babbage again, ". . . the whole of the developments and operations of analysis are now capable of being executed by machinery." Although Babbage was never able to implement this grandiose claim, except in small working models, his proposals were sound and it took over 100 years of engineering progress before they could be practicably transformed into hardware.

The use of holes punched into paper tape for telegraphic transmission was initiated in 1858 by Emile Baudot, who invented a teleprinter that used five magnets to select the character to be printed. His new telegraph code, comprising five equal-length signals, replaced the Morse code of dots and dashes. The 32 combinations of five holes or no-holes (bauds) in paper tape formed the Baudot code, which after modifications (including the provision of seven- or eight-

---

[1] A model built later from Babbage's drawings is in the London Science Museum. Another is on display at the Smithsonian Institution in Washington, D.C.

hole positions per character) became the teletype code now in general use.

The first actual data processing use of punched cards on a significant scale came with the processing of the 1890 federal census data by Herman Hollerith's Electric Tabulating System. The 1880 census had required seven and a half years to process, so that its results were obsolete long before they were tabulated. The 1890 census required only one-third the time. Hollerith had divided his cards into 240 areas, each of which represented a specific census item, such as age, sex, income, and, if punched, would have a fixed meaning as the cards were read by electromechanical sensing devices and their information listed. The punched-card concept spread rapidly, and by World War II, IBM and its chief competitor, Remington, later to become Univac, had built up large punched-card-equipment businesses.

In the 1930s, digital computation techniques using telephone relays[2] were perfected at Bell Telephone Laboratories. Thus, Dr. George R. Stibitz used telephone relays to build a circuit that did additions. And, as the relays became quite reliable, Samuel B. Williams designed and constructed in 1939 the semiautomatic Bell Model I Calculator. This early computing device was used in the design of telephone transmission networks and transformers. Improved models of Bell calculators were constructed later to aid the war effort. The last, Bell Model VI, incorporated self-checking and error-detection circuitry and had an impressive record of error-free calculations.

The highest stage of development of relay computers was represented by the two relay calculators built at Harvard University—Mark I, completed in 1944, and Mark II, about two years later. This activity was spearheaded by Professor Howard H. Aiken. Mark I resulted from a cooperative effort between Harvard's Computation Laboratory and IBM. Its many relays for performance of basic arithmetic operations were controlled by loops of punched IBM card stocks whose punched symbols could represent complete sets or sequences of instructions, and could automatically regulate the shifts of control from one loop to another. Mark I could not, however, "operate" upon its own instructions, or automatically change the course of computation as the result of intermediate calculations.

[2] A relay is a device using an electromagnet, armature, and spring contacts for sensing currents or a voltage in one circuit and passing current in another circuit. The fastest response time is about one millisecond.

Mark I accepted input data on punched cards. Output was on punched cards or printed out on an electric typewriter. Multiplication time was about 4.5 seconds. The device was used extensively by the Navy and represents a major step forward in the development of computers. Its use served to emphasize the need for yet better and faster machines.

During World War II the Army Ordnance Corps badly needed an efficient method of calculating tables of trajectories and firing tables. A group of engineers and mathematicians at the Moore School of Electrical Engineering of the University of Pennsylvania, led by John W. Mauchly and J. Presper Eckert, Jr., offered to design and construct a calculator for this purpose. To speed up the work, it was proposed that only proven components and circuits at conservative tolerances be used. The machine would thus be built entirely with existing "state of the art" techniques. However, the war ended before the machine was completed. ENIAC (*Electronic Numerical Integrator And Calculator*) was delivered at the U.S. Army's Aberdeen Proving Grounds in 1946, where it was successfully operated for 10 years. ENIAC is now at the Smithsonian Institution, where it is displayed as the first true electronic, general-purpose digital computer, the precursor of all that was to come by way of the computer.

DEVELOPMENT OF PUNCHED CARDS

The punched card, invented in 1801 and first used for data processing in 1890, has obviously been with us for a long time, and many manufacturers of computers and related equipment have made it their goal to replace punched cards by other data processing media. Their success has been surprisingly limited. Punched cards, thanks to their economy and flexibility, are still a major means for entering information into computers—particularly for small installations whose volume may not justify magnetic tape drives. In the United States alone, there are nearly 500,000 keypunch units now being used to enter information into cards. Most belong to IBM, and, having long since been amortized, they are probably far more profitable for the company than many of its latest, most futuristic, computer models.

Processing of punched-card information is also still carried out extensively on unit-record equipment, as was done before computers came into use. The role of these installations is declining because of rising labor costs and falling computer costs. However, an examination of their procedures and of the basic principles of the punched card are rewarding, as they provide a simple illustration of some of the basic functions computers perform.

A punched card contains holes that represent information. Standardized locations along the length of the card correspond to the characters of each record in sequence, and one or more holes across its width represents a numerical or alphabetical character, or a special symbol. Figure 3-2 shows a standard 80-column card, with arrays of

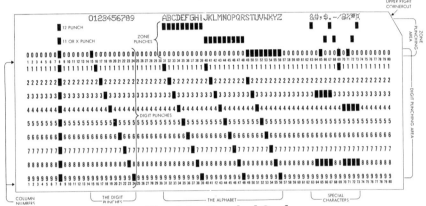

Fig. 3-2. Punched Card

digital (numeric) punches in columns 15 through 24, alphabetic characters in columns 31 through 56, and special symbols in columns 63 through 72.

A typical unit-record installation might include one or more of the following units:

Keypunch	for initial preparation of cards
Verifier	to check that cards have been properly punched
Interpreter	to print out punched information on cards
Sorter	for ordering cards, numerically or alphabetically
Gangpunch	for transferring information from card to card, and for reproducing new cards
Tabulator	for preparing printed copy from information cards, with class totals
Collator	for merging ordered sets of cards, or for dividing one set into several sets
Multiplier (or calculating punch)	for performance of simple calculations and punching out result cards.

A typical application for such an installation would be the ordering and placing in alphabetical or numerical sequence of a large series of names, numbers, or words. This is a common requirement of telephone book publishers, personnel managers, editorial researchers, and so on. In the performance of this message-ordering task, the sorter would rearrange the cards according to their information. Because the sorter operates by sensing one column at a time, in processing numerical data, the complete set of cards must be "passed" as many times as the number of digits in the information field. Alphabetical information would require two passes per column because each alphabetic character is coded by two punches instead of one, doubling sorting time. For example, if the information field were a five-digit number code representing, say, the employee number, ordering the entire deck of cards would require five passes through the sorter. For a code of alphabetic characters or mixed alphabetic and numeric characters, each alphabetic character would require an additional pass. After the cards are ordered, they are passed through the tabulator, which prints page copy showing the desired information, with totals and subtotals of selected classes of data.

COMPUTER CHARACTERISTICS

In contrast to earlier devices, the computer requires no manual intercession after problem statement and data input. The same machine can handle several unrelated problems as long as the instructions for the handling of each problem have been prepared and problem data is available. The computer is distinguished by five specific characteristics:

1. Electronic speed
2. Flexible, elemental instruction set
3. Automatic operation
4. Ability to modify its operations based on intermediate results
5. Versatility

Some of these features have been available with other types of equipment, but only the computer incorporates all of them. Furthermore, no other device possesses the computer's ability to modify its operations in midstream.

The first characteristic, electronic speed, is in itself remarkable. The first computer (ENIAC) operated at speeds measured in milliseconds (thousandths of a second). Today's models routinely operate at speeds rated in nanoseconds (billionths of a second), and speeds rated in picoseconds (trillionths of a second) are now in sight.

The computer's second characteristic, its flexible, elemental instruction set, is related to its first characteristic, speed. Computer instructions are basic, logical building blocks. In their case, "flexible" refers to the capability of grouping different instructions in an almost unlimited number of ways to achieve different results. "Elemental" refers to the simplicity of the individual operations. Since the instructions are logically simple, they are also versatile, but must be used in large numbers if the machine is to perform any useful work because each instruction covers only a very small fragment of the task at hand. With individual instructions taking only several microseconds (millionths of a second) or even nanoseconds of computer time, many thousands of instructions can be carried out to perform each job or solve each problem.

An example of an elemental instruction is: *clear the accumulator, then add into it the number now residing in storage location.* Another example is: *shift one position leftward the digits of the number in the accumulator.* The first computers could perform a surprising variety of tasks with only very few instructions. SEAC ([National Bureau of Standards] Eastern Automatic Computer), the first computer to be put into practical use in the United States, had a repertoire of only eight instructions. Univac, the first computer to become commercially available, had very few more.

The third, and vital, characteristic, automatic operation, is not unique to computers. It should be pointed out here that automatic operation does not mean that any problem, of any complexity, of any size, can be simply put in the hopper and entered into the computer for instant solution. Instead, the job must not exceed the computer's capabilities—speed, storage capacity, logic power (sophistication of instruction set), and so on. The process of estimating whether a particular job can be done on a particular computer system as is, or whether it must be or can be done in a less ambitious form, or in stages, is one that can require considerable time and expertise.

The ability to modify its own operations, based on intermediate results, is the fourth distinguishing characteristic of the computer and the one that truly sets it apart from all other machines. To perform this modification, the computer must be able to test for an intermediate result, and then choose the subsequent direction of its operations. The mechanisms to accomplish this vary according to computer models. However, all include one or more special instructions, called "branch" or "discriminate" instructions. Such an instruction would be preceded in a program by arithmetic steps to produce a numerical value, such as zero or a negative quantity. The testing would then involve: (1) circuitry for sensing such a value ("Is the number in the accumulator zero?" or "Is the number in the accumulator a negative quantity?") and (2) the ability to alter the normal instruction sequence by selecting the next instruction to be executed from another part of internal storage, depending on the test outcome. Of course, the programmer creating the complete set of preplanned instructions would have taken into account all possible contingencies that could arise, and would have devised sets, or "routines" of instructions, to deal with such eventualities, including the placing of these routines in storage.

The last characteristic, versatility, actually represents the sum of all the computer's capabilities. Thanks to this combination, the computer can perform tasks of all types—from solving complex scientific problems to routine payroll bookkeeping—with equal efficiency, as long as they are within the scope of its physical capabilities. Without this versatility, the computer's powers would effectively be wasted much of the time.

Versatility also extends to the computer's basic modes of operations—*off-line* and *on-line*. A computer operates off-line when it works independently of its external environment. It handles each job without interruption from beginning to end, and, serially, in the order in which the job is queued, awaiting processing. The computer's processing speed thus bears no direct relation to that with which information goes in and out of the system. As data for each job to be handled in this mode usually comes in in a single lot or batch, off-line processing is also frequently called *batch processing*.

A computer operating on-line interacts intimately with its external environment, handling queries and other requests for data nearly instantaneously. The effect is that of a conversation between man and computer. Usually the querier uses a terminal of some sort, ranging from a simple teletype to a complex and sophisticated video terminal. Access to the computer may be available to from one to several hundred terminals simultaneously, depending on the system's characteristics. When more than one terminal can have simultaneous access, the computer operates in a *time-sharing* mode. In effect, it divides each minute of its work time into a myriad of tiny segments, interleaving those it devotes to time-shared communications, with those in which it continues to perform regularly assigned tasks. As time-shared operations invariably involve the use of telecommunications, it is important not to confuse them with another operating mode, *remote batch*. This is the teletransmission of batched information for serial processing.

Without versatility, the computer would just be a better machine. With versatility, it becomes (or can become) a partner of man in improving human civilization.

4

The Interface Phenomenon

Computers do many things today that would otherwise be beyond the power of man. They control huge factories with the same unfailing efficiency as that with which they guide space flights or the trajectories of missiles and antimissiles. They perform gigantic calculations and solve complex problems with the same speed with which they pick a wanted man's name from massive files of criminal suspects, or see to the bookkeeping of thousands of savings and loan institutions —and few major banks, businesses, or, for that matter, governments could stay in business today without them. Yet, all of these applications, all of these things, that computers can do are based upon one single feature that is incorporated in the design of computer systems— their information processing capability.

The actual mechanics of computerized information processing are, of course, tremendously complex. However, as is usually the case with complex technologies, the basic principle is a very simple one. In its simplest form, a computer system:

Accepts information in various forms from many sources. In the process, this information is converted into a format that the computer can use.

Processes the information logically so as to provide any or all of the desired problem-solving answers that can be derived from the data at hand, calling, if need be, for additional data.

Outputs the answers or desired listings in a format specified and readable by the human beings or machines (including other computers) who or that will use the information.

This is the chief strength of the computer, but it is a tremendous one—and this is so not only because of all the many things that the computer can do, but because of the extent to which, in doing so, it duplicates a basic natural phenomenon.

Every living organism is an information processing system, a communications system, that maintains its high level of activity only by receiving, storing, retrieving, and acting on information. The criteria that biologists use to determine that an organism is a living one are: irritability, or the ability to react to stimuli; growth, or the ability to increase in size; and reproductivity, or the ability to produce more of its own kind. Each of these criteria assumes some information processing by the organism. Information processed in every organism comes from four primary sources:

Ancestral, phylogenetic, transmitted through the genetic code

Individual, ontogenetic, from experience stored and retrieved—memory

Current endogenous or exogenous experience

Feedback from the organism's monitoring of its own behavior

These information processes probably occur in every structure and function of the organism, for function and structure are merely different aspects of the same processes: one does not exist without the other.

Every cell in a body processes information in a continuous interactive feedback relation with, quite probably, every other cell in the body. The information thus exchanged helps maintain the organism in a favorable state relative to both its internal and external environments. Biologists call the first phenomenon *homeostasis*, the second, *behavior*. In the course of their evolution, organisms develop increasingly greater abilities for acquiring information and suitably coding it. They thus become increasingly able to adapt to or survive in improbable conditions. In fact, evolution is very much the maximization of the improbable. As Dr. Emmanuel Peterfreund has put it: "Information has selective power. It can select or specify one particular configuration out of an ensemble of many configurations that are more or less equally probable. Information is therefore related to biological order. Thus 160 pounds of atoms and molecules can be arranged in an almost infinite variety of ways, but a human being results from a selection of only a very few of the total number of possible arrangements. It is for this reason that life is a most improbable event. . . . Organisms that are progressively higher on the evolutionary scale are progressively more complex, and are therefore more improbable. In other words, the complexity of living forms does not happen by chance."[1]

The directions for creating any organism are contained in four nitrogenous bases—adenine, guanine, thymine, and cytosine. The various arrangements of these four bases constitute the code of life, carrying the blueprint containing the instructions for the development of each organism. The genetic code represents the way in which a sequence of four nitrogenous bases determines the sequence of 20 amino acids. The sequence of these amino acids in turn determines the kinds of building blocks, the proteins, of the organism. Just as 26 letters of the alphabet make many different languages possible, four nitrogenous bases strung in their thousands of different sequences along each strand of the double helix of the DNA molecule containing the genetic code make many kinds of life possible.[2] But only one of those sequences, only one of those kinds of life, is that of man.

THE NATURE OF INTERFACE

Man's evolutionary history appears to be based on the hazard that, in his case, enforced a particular configuration of the DNA molecule. Indeed, this chance event has been the prime mover through most of

---

[1] Emmanuel Peterfreund, *Information, Systems and Psychoanalysis* (New York: International Universities Press, 1971), p. 118.

[2] For a fuller treatment of this subject, see Ashley Montagu, *Human Heredity*, 2d ed. (New York: World Publishing Co., 1963), pp. 26-41; and Max Levitan and Ashley Montagu, *Textbook of Human Genetics* (New York: Oxford University Press, 1971).

his evolution into a semblance of true humanity. But once that point was reached, there came a new phenomenon. *Homo faber,* man the maker, was created, and man was no longer helplessly adrift on the waves of genetic evolution. Instead, his development now depended on the success with which he adapted to new and different environments, relying on new behavior patterns that he either had derived from his surroundings or had himself completely created.

Man the maker has been busily making himself—and, in doing so, he has made himself even more "improbable" a creature than any other that has ever existed on this earth. The man-made (learned) part of the environment that man has created, into which he has moved, is his culture. Culture is the storehouse of experience that enables man to control, modify, and change his environment.

Man's interactions with his environment have an interesting similarity to the physical and chemical phenomenon known as "interface." In the inanimate world, interface is defined as "a surface regarded as the common boundary of two bodies or spaces." The meaning of this term can be readily extended to embrace similar boundary phenomena in living things, and in the encounters of man with his environment.

In the course of his cultural evolution, man has obviously become increasingly complex. This complexity has been reflected, sometimes even exaggerated, in his relationship to his environment—and in man's requirement for ever more powerful information processing capabilities with which to keep up with this complexity. Thus the computer is an inevitable end product of the search for a synthetic extension of the human mind. The computer better helps man to explore the nature of the interface phenomena that govern his relationships to his surroundings. And, once these interface phenomena are understood, they can be controlled. In this way, the computer enables man to react more constructively to his environment and makes him better able to modify and to master it.

Examples of interface phenomena abound in the everyday world of physical objects—plants, animals, things. The characteristics of familiar substances go unnoticed by most of us, but not by the scientists who must classify and measure their properties, such as hardness, smoothness, porosity, plasticity, surface tension, and so on. In many situations, elaborate adjustments or precautions must be taken to protect or insure people or their creations against damage or destruction related to interface. For example, coverings, wrappings, and other claddings must be used for waterproofing, temperature control, and shockproofing, to compensate for interface situations inadequately protected from nature. Thus, the shock that we receive from handling an uninsulated electric wire is definitely an interface phenomenon. Such precautions are particularly important to protect people and objects who will experience unfamiliar surroundings or physical conditions whose interface characteristics are, accordingly, little known.

Interface takes on additional special significance in the engineer's world of electrical and electronic circuits. Moving parts in machinery are designed to minimize energy losses due to friction.[3] Although not a literal example of interface in Webster's sense, transformation of energy from one form to another represents an interface phenomenon, and one costly in lost energy. For example, substantial amounts of energy are lost in the change of mechanical to electrical power in a generator. At the other end of the cycle, an electric motor delivers less motive power than the equivalent electrical powering input. In most such situations, the start-up losses are greater than the steady-state losses. This corresponds electrically to the phenomenon of inertia in purely mechanical systems.

Inertia is the resistance of matter to changes in its state of motion. Galileo's discovery of the principle of inertia is said to have laid the foundation for the science of mechanics. Isaac Newton's first law of classical mechanics restates the same principle: that objects at rest remain at rest, and objects in motion remain in uniform linear motion. It is well known that it takes much more energy to move a heavy object from a resting position than it does to keep it moving, once started. Electrical power designs have long included special features to supply such "surges" of power. Also, sources of electrical power must provide reserves to cover surge-energy requirements. These costly requirements reflect the pervasive and varying effects of interface phenomena in all of our lives.

HOW COMPUTERS INTERFACE

An interface of another sort becomes apparent in the sophisticated world of special- and general-purpose electronic systems. It becomes manifest at the points of contact between different communications

---

[3] Not always an undesirable phenomenon: We don rubber overshoes to *add* friction at the interface between shoe sole and wet or icy ground.

media. For example, the electronic circuits in computers operate at speeds so high that special arrangements must be made to accommodate information input and output that proceed at far slower rates. For this reason, these interfaces are perhaps better characterized as points of "speed change"—the points of interconnection between input devices reading data at, say, 100 characters per second and high-speed computer storage with cycle speeds of over 100,000 characters per second. This transition requires a buffer, or temporary storage, capable of accepting data at the inputting device's rate, accumulating it until there is a full "buffer load" to be inputted to the computer at its speed. This interface is analogous to the point of contact between two runners in a relay race who must run at approximately the same speed before they can transfer the relay token from one to the other. In practice, in many computer system installations, a great number of malfunctions occur at just such an interface—more frequently than at any interface point in the system where data or signal transfers take place at constant speeds. Similarly, provisions must be made for buffering of output data to allow efficient transfer of digital data to the slower-speed output devices—printers, magnetic tapes and disk drives, card punches, and so on—from computer memory.

Computer interface situations also occur outside the system, such as at the point where information is converted from human readable to machine readable. Here the interface is provided by the human transcriber of data, the operator of a keypunch or keytape device, for example, who reads data on worksheets and enters it onto punched cards or magnetic tape. There is a complex interaction between human and mechanical components—cognitive processes, language and cultural backgrounds in symbol usage, and the relatively rigid and primitive state of development of the electromechanical devices involved. Prior to being transcribed, the material must be prepared—identification and editing symbols annotated, along with abbreviations and codes, and the whole standardized, and so on. The equipment used by the operator, including the desk and chair, requires constant maintenance. In addition, suitable working conditions—lighting, comfort, rest break—must be provided. Finally, arrangements must be made to handle the operator's production, including error checking, and batching of output, storage, and workload adjustments to smooth out the flow of work. Transformation of raw data from human- to machine-readable form thus involves a combination of various types of interface, including interfacing between human beings and between human beings and inanimate objects and machines.

HUMAN INTERFACES

Let us look at a few common examples of human interface. A newborn baby's first contacts with the world outside the womb comprise a succession of crises to be met and overcome. He must learn to use his physical senses of touch, taste, and smell almost immediately after birth. As they serve his biological needs successfully, and as they are repeatedly experienced, coordinated muscular and brain-record patterns are created and stored. These patterns are subsequently brought ever more easily into play when the proper occasions occur. As he grows, the child experiences other interfacing situations—with nature, with people, with mechanical devices—and each contact leaves its imprint on his emerging personality and character.

Although the details of personality formation may never be fully understood, it is likely that a first occurrence of a particular kind of contact has more impact than succeeding occurrences of the same type. For example, the first time a child encounters a new teacher in his first school experience is undoubtedly far more significant in influencing his attitudes relating to authority in general than later meetings with the same teacher or initial contacts with other teachers. The class of interfaces between a person and inanimate objects can be represented by the example of a child's first experiences with the phenomenon of gravity—the first time he falls out of bed, or notices the rain, or sees leaves falling from a tree, or is hit by an object that falls from above. Of course, other examples, such as a child's first burn from touching a hot object, or a cut or injury from sharp edges, represent dramatic interfaces with the world around him.

Differences in home environment among children who come together for their first experiences away from home—in nursery school or kindergarten—bring out another variation of interface in personal relationships. Parents' personal attitudes and habits and their efforts to instill them in growing children vary greatly. The home atmosphere—religious training, habits of speech, interpersonal behavior, moral attitudes, artistic interests, and the like—not only is reflected in the image each child presents to others, but forms the basis for a real broadening influence as he is made aware of the differences in the backgrounds of other children. Very probably, also, such opportunities for children to "compare notes" with each other become eye-opening realizations of their own parents' faults—traumatic discoveries that their mothers and fathers are fallible.

Maturing and adult individuals experience interface phenomena as they assume responsibility for their own actions. Holding down a job, particularly one's first job, requires a variety of contacts with people, and variations in coping can spell success or failure. Very frequently, personality traits count quite as much as job performance. "Ability to get along" can usually be differentiated at three different levels of relationships. They are, very simply, relations with people "up," "across," and "down." That is, relations toward one's superiors, toward colleagues, and toward one's subordinates. We are all familiar with the type of supervisor whose primary interest seems to be to make a good showing for *his* boss, while being stern and repressive to his own subordinates. Probably just as familiar is the type at the other extreme, who is especially kind to his employees, who wants to be liked—sometimes at the expense of maintaining proper discipline. For both these extremes, and for many types of individuals whose personality traits fall in between, there may be "people contacts" that are particularly traumatic. One such "interface" may be the occasion of one's being required to deliver an important verbal report to high-ranking officials. Again, for most of us, the task of notifying an employee that he is to be discharged, or the necessity of rebuking one, can be a trying experience. Another situation, involving neither an "up" nor a "down" relationship, might be the need to present an unpopular position in behalf of one's organization at a meeting with competing organizations.

The average citizen, whether living in an urban or rural environment, is today involved, directly or indirectly, in a bewildering complex of relationships. He is expected to be many things: subordinate worker, cohort, husband, associate, son, father, friend to the various people with whom he interacts (interfaces). Many examples could be cited of organizations he might belong to: union, church, political party, hobby group, and so on. In fact, it is entirely possible for some individuals to be affiliated with two or more organizations that are often necessarily on opposite sides of a particular issue. For example, a member of a certain labor union may also own stock in a corporation whose management finds itself at odds with the same union. If he is an active working member in either or both conflicting parties, he may suffer conflict.

Even without formally joining any organization, each citizen is involved, as an individual and also as part of one or more segments of society, in relationships that force him to play a role. As a taxpayer he has two or more levels of interaction that directly affect his pocket. Besides local, state, and federal income taxes, there are property, school, excise, and other direct taxes, plus sales tax, and fees for water, sewer, and other municipal services. As a law-abiding citizen, he is assumed to be fully knowledgeable about all laws. He is therefore responsible both on his own account and for members of his family for obeying the law and suffering the consequences of violations. In today's motor-vehicle-dominated society, a citizen's most frequent encounter with "the law" is apt to be through the traffic regulations or as a result of auto accidents. And because conflicts with other citizens or businesses are inevitable, the citizen is apt to appear in the law courts as defendant or as plaintiff, with consequent emotional strain and expense almost inevitable. And, for those citizens who are also parents, there are all the prideful and worrisome aspects of that awesome responsibility: providing a loving home atmosphere, by feeding, clothing, educating, disciplining, protecting, guiding, leading, and most of all, loving.

We could go on and on with the cataloging of the typical individual's involvements—we have already touched on some of these. Nearly all require more or less intimate contacts with other persons or groups, and, in each, a judgment or assessment by the individual of degree of support or conflict. Is the contact friendly? Can I believe what he says? Should I agree or disagree with this policy? Should I buy what they're trying to sell me? What will my wife (husband) think? Can I get that job for the boss done in time? Will the boss recommend me for promotion?

INTERFACING WITH TECHNOLOGY

In this chapter we have seen that man's history is largely that of his increasing involvement and interaction with his environment in order to control it. And, in mankind's drive for control of its surroundings, the biggest obstacles, the major problems have been those resulting from interface phenomena—the difficulties that occur when we must deal with physical laws or inanimate objects, or, and this may be most difficult of all, strive to establish understanding among ourselves. Our chief tool in dealing with these problems has been our expanding technology—even though, in the course of its expansion, it may create or uncover even more physical and human problems than it solves.

The computer is the latest and the most powerful of our technological tools. To understand fully what its role can be in our society, it would be well to examine briefly the extent to which technology has already affected the basic physical aspects of our lives. These aspects formerly dealt with our survival, but now chiefly concern our contentment. However, they still represent those areas where we remain most vulnerable to hard-to-predict interface difficulties—those caused by nature, or by ourselves. These are the areas against whose dangers we must use the computer's powers as we have used all previous tools of our technology.

The basic physical needs of man come under at least three traditional headings: food, shelter, and clothing.

FOOD.   The production of food by farming is one of the few activities that, in many regions, still remains to be mechanized. The small farmer can still tend a herd of cows, milk by hand, till the soil using nothing more elaborate than a hoe, pick vegetables, fruit, cotton, and berries by hand, and shear wool from a small flock of sheep. The Amish settlements in Pennsylvania constitute examples of holdovers from earlier times, employing only hand tools, and equipment no more complex than can be driven by wind or water or drawn by horses. But the Amish are only the exception to the general practice, since most farms are now thoroughly mechanized, and, in fact, large growers could not survive without the aid of machines. In 1970, fewer than 7 million farm workers were feeding over 200 million Americans. In 1910, it took nearly 19 million farmers to feed a U.S. population of 92 million.

Paradoxically, the desire to improve agricultural techniques ultimately led man to the 18th-century Industrial Revolution. That remarkable century, following upon the great discoveries of the preceding century, of Newton, Harvey, Galileo, Leibnitz, Kepler, Boyle, and others, was much taken with the practical application of those discoveries. Physical models for human conduct and social control flourished. The philosophical speculations of Descartes and Locke, combined with the physical theories of the 17th-century savants, led to such works as La Mettrie's *Man a Machine* (Leyden, 1748), and to François Quesnay's physiocratic writings on animal and human economy, the *Essai Physique sur l'Economie Animale* (Paris, 1736), and the *Tableau Economique* (Versailles, 1758). According to La Mettrie, all the human faculties—emotion, imagination, judgment, memory— are, like sensations, simply material manifestations. The same determinism that governs the movements of matter also controls the manifestations of the spirit or soul. The physiocrats held that in economic as in animal society, organic life was self-perpetuating. Just as Harvey had demonstrated that the blood circulates systemically through the body nourishing its tissues and organs, yielding some of its ingredients and taking up others, returning to the heart and lungs to be replenished, so the wealth of society is replenished through production, exchange, and distribution in a strictly natural, harmonious manner. The setting in which economic laws work is natural, and its foundation is agriculture, for agriculture is the sole source of wealth. The poor, it was held, are necessary to cooperate with nature in making its wealth available, by extracting it from the soil so that it can be converted into consumable form.[4]

In 18th-century Europe scientific investigation led to improved systems for tilling, bettering livestock, and otherwise raising yield. The invention of machines for spinning and weaving began the new production trend that culminated in the factory system, and undoubtedly was partly the result of a need to accommodate the greater yields from the new agriculture. Like a vicious cycle, the new factories stimulated still more farming improvements, which partly took the form of more and more inventions of direct aid in farming and food production. The improved plow, invented by John Deere, and the machines for tilling, harvesting, baling, and the like made it practical to operate large farms.

Today it is almost inconceivable that we can satisfy the world's agricultural needs without massive use of machines at all levels: production, processing, preservation, storage, transport, and of course packaging, marketing, and distribution. As an example, the poultry industry has become so highly developed that huge incubating, hatching, feeding, and egg-collecting equipment can be operated almost

---

4 For a valuable discussion of the subject, see Leonora Cohen Rosenfield, *From Beast-Machine to Man-Machine* (New York: Oxford University Press, 1941).

without human intervention. In almost every aspect of farming, the modern farm operator uses machinery and mechanisms, from tractor-driven equipment in the field to refrigeration, heating, and food processing and packing equipment.

Particularly in the preparation, preservation, and packing activities, large industries have grown up. Canned and frozen foods, and many varieties of other "convenience foods" have in recent years, and particularly in the United States, come to represent a growing part of the typical shopper's budget.

SHELTER.   Like food, shelter represents one of mankind's traditional basic needs. Through the ages, man has exhibited ingenuity and resourcefulness in providing himself with comfortable housing. After early man's natural refuge—the cave—came the lean-to, wigwam, log cabin, frame, stone, and brick houses—all examples of man's use of materials around him.

The use of machinery in home construction did not begin to have a noticeable impact until power tools became widely available after World War II. Power tools transformed the lumber industry overnight by making available standardized boards, trim, and fittings. Production of plywood and a variety of pressed-composition panels has been another result of the combination of new materials technology with power tools and factory production techniques. Other new materials and construction techniques have been under steady development ever since.

The next stage in the home-building revolution is the natural result of tendencies toward standardization and efforts to intensify the use of factory techniques—the prefabricated homes and prefabricated sections industry. Prefabricated houses and entire high-rise buildings have become common in Europe. In the United States, possibly because of opposition by trade unions and the inflexibility of local construction codes, acceptance is coming about more slowly.

CLOTHING.   The origins of the 18th-century Industrial Revolution go back to the invention of spinning and weaving machines. The sewing machine was invented in the latter part of the 18th century by an Englishman named Thomas Saint, but the first practical machines did not appear until about 1850, when Elias Howe and Isaac M. Singer brought out workable models. Specialized versions for leather work, buttonholes, and other purposes were also developed.

During the mid-19th century, machines for the production of clothing came into wide use. Factory production of clothing in a great variety of sizes and styles now almost exclusively dominates the clothing industry, which of course utilizes many specialized machines and tools. We are now accustomed to referring to clothes made in the home with electric-powered sewing machines as "hand sewn." Along with the typewriter and the automobile, the sewing machine has become one of a relatively small group of machines of which the average citizen is both owner and trained operator. In these cases, machines have become members of the family, in effect, and are intimately involved in habit patterns.

HOME MANAGEMENT.   Along with the three traditional necessities of life—food, shelter, and clothing—there is a fourth aspect of the machine's effects on man, in the area of "home management." Here, man's relations with technology are manifested at several levels, according to the degree of conscious user involvement. Machines used to perform household tasks belong to one of three more-or-less overlapping categories: automatic, semiautomatic, and user operated. Examples of machines generally available in typical middle-income modern American homes are listed in table 4-1, which shows the user-involvement category for each. It is seen that several overlap categories. For example, some models of cameras are equipped with automatic light meter and focusing, making picture taking practically automatic. Similarly, some record players may be loaded with enough records to play continuously for many hours, while others are manually operated. Lawn mowers and vacuum cleaners are classified as user operated, although experimental machines have been tested that would operate entirely automatically, under control of photoelectric devices to sense obstructions and control steering.

Home managers are being provided with devices that incorporate an increasing degree of automation, performing their tasks with a minimum of human intervention. The simple rheostat that maintains home temperatures at a steady level has been with us for a long time, but it still requires human settings. Temperature controls being developed today can be programmed for self-sufficiency, acting on information provided by instruments that sense both internal home temperatures and outside climate conditions. Similarly, grandmother's coal range, which had not a speck of automation, has been replaced by a wall-mounted, eye-level oven that turns itself off when

TABLE 4-1   Machines in Home Management
Showing User Involvement

	Auto-matic	Semi-Auto-matic	User Operated
Home heating, thermostat equipped	x		
Hot water heater	x		
Automatic washer	x		
Washer with wringer		x	x
Telephone		x	
Refrigerator	x		
Sewing machine			x
Typewriter			x
Food mixer		x	x
Electric or gas oven	x	x	
Surface cooking unit		x	x
Television		x	
Record Player	x	x	x
Automobile			x
Camera		x	x
Garage door opener	x		
Power lawn mower			x
Vacuum cleaner			x
Home workshop			x

the roast is done, and may even whistle "Dixie." Some experimental models can even be turned on and off via telephone.

The computer's role in the home is still very limited, if it exists at all. There have, for instance, been tests of remote computerized readings of water and gas meters. However, its domestic role will undoubtedly emerge in the next two decades—both in the form of miniaturized "black boxes" that will control basic household requirements, such as heating and air conditioning, and through remote services of all sorts, including information accounting and instructions, available through visual display terminals.

THE COMPUTER AT THE THRESHOLD

The computer is so powerful and its presence so pervasive that it is easy to forget how comparatively recent is its widespread usage. There are still many areas of human activity where the computer is just starting to be used to its full potential. Where and when this occurs, many new demands are placed on the people affected. New applications must be developed; additional training is required. Things must be done in different ways and the results judged by different standards.

The introduction of the computer frequently causes many stresses, but there are very real reasons why such problems should be treated differently from those caused by other machines. The latter handle things, while the computer deals with information and ideas. Consequently, members of an organization, from top managers down to the most junior employees, find it difficult to grasp exactly how the computer affects them personally, though they know that they are affected. This requires suitable training, indoctrination, or just adequate explanations when a computer is to be installed, or the operations of one already on-site are to be substantially modified.

A great deal of preparation must be made when the computer is at the threshold, when its role in the operations of an organization is about to be greatly expanded. For many public and private concerns, this has often meant a top-to-bottom review of management and record-keeping procedures. Frequently, the resulting changes in procedures improved and streamlined the organization's operations, quite independently of computerization. Management's interface with the computer can thus provide it with an evaluation of its own maturity—a measure of management's understanding of its own operations.

5

When Knowledge Is Wealth

A constant feature of human culture over most of the past 4,000 years has been man's search for a safe, standardized, easily transferable symbol for the value of physical objects, which could be readily exchanged for them. Today, we call this symbol money and we think of it in terms of bills and coins, even if inflation does make us somewhat doubtful of their value. There have been other symbols used in man's antiquity. Bars of precious metals, cattle, seashells, certified virgins, pedigreed bulls, and working wives—all of these, and more, have been used in their time, in their place, to symbolize wealth. All have failed. They have failed to retain their value or to keep it at all. All of them—no longer scarce metals, cattle starved by drought, deflowered virgins, or the currency of defeated nations—have ceased to symbolize wealth in the eyes of men, or even of their possessors.

Only one commodity has always retained worth—information. Quickly obsoleted, difficult to quantify and standardize, hence never used as a unit of exchange, information has still increasingly come to represent the true wealth of society, and its development and processing is one of society's chief tasks.

There is nothing really new in this. All human societies have been information processing societies or systems. And, if these societies were poor, as most of them have been, it was because they were such poor information processing systems. The progress in processing information that man has made on his way to civilization has been largely planless, frequently achieved through accident and serendipity.

Discoveries of crucial importance for man's development have been repeatedly neglected and forgotten and, when rediscovered, have been described as having originally been either "before" or "ahead" of their time. This, of course, is ridiculous. No discovery is ahead of its time rather than a product of it. Instead, it is people without vision who are *behind* their time—people who resist change and who frequently mistake their beliefs for the laws of nature.

Charles Babbage, who conceived the first true computer, was a man of his time. Living at the impetuous beginning of the Industrial Revolution, when the science of mathematics was expanding as never before, he was well aware of what his device could do in the world he lived in. Despite initial government backing, he failed to build a computer. What defeated him was the failure of the contemporary metalworking technology to live up to the time—the failure of this technology to keep pace with the development of other technologies so as to give them adequate support. It was behind the time.

This tendency to resist change is evident in all societies and at all times. It is as basic as the homeostatic phenomenon common to all living organisms, the tendency of each organism to strive to maintain steady and positive conditions. At the physiological level, certain human bodily functions tend to remain constant—for instance, man's "normal" temperature of 98.6 degrees, the balance of oxygen and carbon dioxide in the bloodstream, glucose level in the blood, and so on. At the total organism level, man strives to maintain and protect himself and his family against threats to the constancy and comfort of their environment—and to his economic well-being, social status, professional standing, and so on. Homeostasis covers the many ways through which the human personality maintains "a pattern of steady states," sometimes even covering attempts to protect these states by modifying the environment.

Individuals and groups react to change in very different ways. Thus, in a culture like ours where "progress" is felt to be almost synonymous with increased comfort or material gain, society is usually able to accept physical innovations and gadgets fairly readily. Other cultures embrace progress with less ease: witness the relative slowness of Britons to accept and install on a large scale central heating and air conditioning. We Americans, on the other hand, are slow to accept changes that affect us emotionally rather than materially. As sociologists point out, our attitudes and institutions lag behind our technology. In short, the various parts of modern culture are not changing at the same rate. According to sociologist William F. Ogburn: "The strain that exists between two correlated parts of culture that change at unequal rates of speed may be interpreted as a lag in the part that is changing at the slowest rate, for the one lags behind the other."[1]

ROUND TWO FOR THE COMPUTER

Most sociologists agree that the computer represents a compound force acting on society—because, while it has produced far-reaching material changes, it has had vast nonmaterial effects as well. It has helped us to vastly increase our material wealth, but even more it has made our society data-rich. It has made us wealthy in knowledge. And, as this wealth has grown, so has the social importance of knowledge. This is evidenced by our steadily rising expenditures for research, development, education, and training ever since World War II. Similarly, the systematic analysis and evaluation of knowledge is becoming increasingly important in decision making by private and public organizations. And the need for better information, as in the case of major defense procurement programs, becomes ever more apparent.

Knowledge means finding new ways to do things that are better than the existing ways. Knowledge thus means change, and the computer therefore represents a powerful agent for change; and its potential for change is increasing all the time. Over the past 12 years, computers have become common throughout the world, doing things that we are seldom aware of in ways that we rarely understand, but we are certain that the end result will affect us personally. However, this has just been "round one." There is a second round coming up, and this time the effect is going to be both far more widespread and more fundamental, for the computer is no longer relegated to a distant computer room. It is now economical and practical to link it via telephone lines to our homes and offices. There, we can have free conversational access to its problem-solving capabilities and stored information through computer terminals—which are increasingly simple to use and a growing number of which are equipped with video displays. The computer is becoming a tool that we, as individuals, can use directly and easily.

Only one of the many predictions made concerning the social effects of the computer's expanded availability is 100 percent certain to come true. Whatever the effects will be, some will certainly be unexpected by the standards of today. One of the more paradoxical examples is provided by the U.S. Army, hardly one of the world's great breeding grounds for radical ideas or novel departures. When large American ground forces were still engaged in combat in Vietnam, it was not uncommon for massive air strikes and artillery barrages to be called in and coordinated by personnel as low in rank as sergeants. In World War II, this would have been a colonel's responsibility, but in past years, the army, using computers, has vastly improved its fire control systems. Thus the creation of these ultrapowerful, centralized systems has resulted in the granting of greater independence and responsibility to lower-ranking personnel, a result that is most unlikely to have been included among the objectives of the system development project.

The expanding availability of computers for use by individuals and the increasing variety of this use will certainly accentuate two of knowledge's basic paradoxes. One is that while knowledge may make us rich and comfortable, it also menaces our wealth and our comfort through the changes that it likewise creates. The second, and more ironic, is that a changing society requires even more new knowledge to protect itself against the unfamiliarity and uncertainty that comes with change. Existing attitudes, knowledge, and institutions can cope only with what is already current. The implementation of new knowledge can be carried through only if we have additional information concerning its potential and its social, economic, and political effects. The role of the computer is to support this cycle of new knowledge, creating requirements for yet newer knowledge. The greater availability of the computer will help us keep up with what is new and what must be known, but it will also speed up the cycle's rate, so that the volume of new knowledge will keep on increasing at a rate that may well outstrip our abilities to assimilate it usefully.

Coping with change does not mean simply establishing a graceful transition from obsolete methods to new ways of doing things. Change also greatly increases the scope and variety of what we can do. This, in turn, means that the number of choices that society must make is greatly expanded, and so is the number of alternate choices from among which the selections must be made. How great is this variety of choices is exemplified in the shifting relationships of political bodies in the nation. Just as a powerful centralized fire control system allowed low-ranked personnel to exercise greater independent responsibility, the increased flow of information generated by computers is making possible the assumption of more authority by lower level political units. Counties, for instance, once dismissed as bucolic relics, are now emerging as major regional government units, sometimes superseding cities in the process. States, seemingly once doomed to subservience to Washington, are reemerging as effective power centers.

The revival of local and state governments appears to have federal support, as evidenced by revenue-sharing proposals. However, a choice has yet to be consciously made as to how power will be distributed in the future among the various levels of government units. This will be a political choice, and as the impact of technology on our society becomes ever greater, major technological issues will increasingly require political solutions. Certainly, in the case of local governments, the question of whether computer communications and techniques allow actions to be independently taken locally, and simultaneously coordinated in a nationwide, real-time monitoring network, may well become a political issue.

COMPUTERS AND POWER

In a data-rich society, knowledge does not merely mean wealth; it also means power. As a result, we are now faced with a very real problem of information power, the problem of how to control the potential inherent in our constantly growing stock of knowledge. This is a brand-new problem, probably going back no further than the start of the computer's second generation, late in the 1960s. It is quite different from previous information-related puzzlers. In the past, information was stored chiefly in books or on film, both forms that imposed a time gap between knowledge and resulting action. This gap was only slightly reduced by radio and then by television. However, the separation between knowledge and action has since been eliminated by the use of on-line, time-sharing computer systems that make it possible for an action to be initiated in the same seconds in which the initiating data are collected and processed. An antimissile missile is set off by a radar reading; a complex balance updating and interest computing procedure is started by a bank teller window deposit; or a massive replenishment order is automatically placed as soon as a company's stock of a certain part or material falls below a present level. In all of these, and many more, cases, there is a dynamic process in which knowledge is expressed as physical action, is expressed as power.

Information power would not have been seen as a problem only a few years ago. Instead, it might have been considered a resounding confirmation of the traditional American confidence in technology as the cure for all ailments. However, this joy has been muted by the realization that information power is far more powerful than its developers had conceived—that its impact is unleashed in ways that are far from clear to us, and with bewildering effects, and that we have yet to find adequate means with which to control this impact (assuming that anyone is seriously trying). Its effects can be seen in every field where a formal structural hierarchy of power has long been in existence—in business where the role of the middle manager and of the top executives are being rapidly altered; in government where, for better or worse, the relationship between federal and lower-level government units is undergoing a gradual revolution; and in world security where, because of the sheer size of the factors involved, the impact's results may be most apparent.

It might have been thought that an increase in the world's stock of knowledge would have been a unifying factor in the world—that international agencies would have been established to speed the interchange of this knowledge, that nations would have been drawn closer by these exchanges, and that at least some of the differences between people and nations would have been erased. This has not been the case. International exchanges of knowledge that could affect national security have been very limited. The unifying effects of information power have been best applied inside nations or power blocs. Major nations, such as the United States, Russia, and China have been able to reduce substantially local differences within their borders. However, knowledge, instead of making national outlooks more similar, has placed them in sharper focus, to delineate how much they differ and to set them further apart from each other. Knowledge has, in that sense, thus served to divide the world into cohesive blocks, rather than unite it. True, the number of the major contending powers is smaller than formerly, but, even because of that, their differences may run far deeper.

We have often heard it said that a nation that can send men to the moon should be capable of down-to-earth accomplishments—that its technological know-how could be applied to the analysis and solution of social problems with the same happy results as were obtained for space problems. We may hear such statements with increasing irony as we reflect on the many paradoxes that have been created as unintended by-products of computer usage. Also, social problems are far more complex than those of space travel. However, some perspective is needed. If solutions to complex special problems are needed, if new democratic procedures are to be developed, it is unlikely that this can be done otherwise than through computers.

Information power may in the future be harnessed through computer testing and simulation of alternative man/machine procedures for management of information for society. The results of these tests will be made public and will be subject to debate before any course is adopted either through the normal political process or through regulation by special agencies. Information power can be controlled for the service of man if men can agree on how and why it should be used.

FUTURE PORTENTS?

Men are already finding that they can agree on the control and use of information power when there are no proprietary economic or national interests involved. Typical examples are provided by libraries and education. Libraries and information centers have steadily expanded their use of computer techniques in cataloging and indexing, and for bibliographic and information retrieval services. To make their limited resources go further and to try to keep up with the fast-growing output of the information and publishing industries, the library and information services have also increased the degree of their cooperation.

As might be expected, leading roles in the development of computerized services have been played by the national libraries: the Library of Congress, the National Library of Medicine, and the National Agricultural Library. Among the developments they have initiated are: standardization of catalog terms and machine codes, dissemination of machine-readable catalog data, establishment of indexes to current scientific literature, and the operation of information retrieval services. Simultaneously, abstracting and indexing of scientific publications, traditionally performed for many scientific disciplines, have been streamlined through computerization. Regional centers or groups of libraries have also been participating increasingly in cooperative efforts to eliminate duplication and permit common use of library materials. As communications and other problems are solved, these sources of information will become increasingly available and accessible to individual citizens and businesses.

In education, computer-assisted learning, also called computer-aided instruction (CAI) is one of several approaches toward the individualization of instruction. In most test CAI applications, the student interacts with the computer through a keyboard terminal, frequently equipped with a visual display. The computer is programmed to "lead the student by the hand" through a given subject, by presenting multiple choice questions and reacting appropriately to the student's replies. The student proceeds at his own pace into progressively more advanced material and by programmed jumps to more difficult questions. If his responses indicate the need, the information is repeated over and over, and he may be referred to additional study material, until he shows sufficient improvement.

The development of CAI has been handicapped by the high cost of equipment, and the technique has proved feasible only when it was implemented by a time-sharing system linked to a large number of terminals. In addition, both the software and the instructional material are still deficient and require careful and extensive development.

Programmed self-instruction textbooks, which use the computer teaching technique without any actual computer hardware, have been published. The basic technique used in these textbooks is the providing of single bits, or frames, of information in logical order to enable the reader to begin with the most rudimentary aspects of a subject and to progress to the more complex at his own speed. Personal study (without using computers) of such texts is quite useful in itself. It, in effect, provides an example of manual simulation of a computer application. As such approaches are perfected, educational methods may be gradually transformed.

WHY COMPUTERS FAIL

The authors of this book and probably every inhabitant of the 50 states and adjacent territories have commented at least once, and with increasing asperity, on computer errors. The device, which is billed everywhere as the ultimate information machine, is also frequently a source of misinformation—as frequently as every time that we receive an incorrect computer-produced bill or read about costly government overspending caused by computer error. The answer as to why this is so is quite simple—very often computers do not work.

> Ironically, the basic problem which the computer poses is inefficiency—because the computer *is* difficult to use. All communications between the user and the machine must first be formalized by large professional staffs of programmers and analysts before the user can achieve the necessary data processing capability at some future date.[2]

This statement, made in 1963, is still substantially true. The computer can function perfectly only when there can be complete and direct communications between the computer and the end user, with the latter using his own words and methods without any constant reference to a set of artificial codes or preset methods and vocabularies for giving instructions to the computer. Much has been done along that line, but the computer is still a very imperfect device, and this is best seen in those areas where computers and human beings must work together, as for instance in systems that are designed primarily to collect, process, and provide up-to-date, rapidly changing action information. These are the systems that will, in the future, help the housewife as well as the managers of giant corporations, and bring the benefits of computer power directly to all individuals.

The chief causes of the frequent failures of information systems have generally been human ones. Computers can automatically take in, process, and store any amount of information, and then disgorge it in any form prescribed by the user and designed to satisfy any variety of specific requirements. This specification is a human responsibility and one that all too often is imperfectly performed because of poor prior analysis of the system. Dr. Simon Ramo, a cofounder of TRW, Inc., has described the importance of the "systems approach" in systems analysis. "It is," he says, "an approach that insists at looking at a problem in its entirety, taking into account all the facts, all the intertwined parameters. . . . indeed, it starts by insisting on a clear

---

[2] Address by Maj. Gen. C. H. Terhune, Jr. to the American Federation of Information Processing Societies, Las Vegas, Nevada, Nov. 12, 1963, Air Force Systems Command, Electronic Systems Division News Release, Office of Information, L. G. Hanscom Field, Bedford, Massachusetts.

understanding of exactly what the problem is and of the goals that should dominate the solution. . . ."[3]

Obviously the systems approach is one that must be instituted at the very start of the systems design process—before a computer is installed, or substantially reconfigured—to take into consideration the tasks that the computer must handle. Edward Tomeski has discussed some of the risks and pitfalls that may crop up whenever there has been a failure to consider all relevant factors prior to the initiation of computer operations. Thousands of computer installations, he says, are of "questionable economic utility."[4] He believes that this is often because of excessive emphasis on hardware and inadequate considerations of other major factors, including the following:

Proper systems planning
Applications analysis and systems design
Staffing, at both the management and analyst levels
Realistic analysis of past and future costs and benefits
Directly relevant peripheral aspects, including software support and delivery schedule, supporting equipment cost and interface, facility planning and cost, preparation of master files and procedures for computer applications
Review and control of systems design, computer programming, testing, debugging, and implementation

The computer is the most powerful tool devised by man the tool-maker, but it is only a tool. Computer errors are human errors.

PLANNING WITH COMPUTERS

Knowledge is information not only about what has happened, but also about what will happen—or, at least, about how to make it happen; in one word, planning. Computers and computer techniques have become the principal tools for the planning and scheduling of major projects—from the construction of an industrial or housing complex to "le Plan," the master plan for the development of France's economy that is drawn up every five years as a guide for all areas of the entire nation's economic and industrial activities.

3 Simon Ramo, *Cure for Chaos* (New York: David McKay Co., 1969).

4 Edward Tomeski, *The Executive Use of Computers* (New York: Collier Books, 1969).

Planning comes close to being a "traditional" computer application. The use of effective computerized planning methods goes back to 1958 when the U.S. Navy introduced PERT (Program Evaluation and Review Technique), developed in conjunction with its Polaris weapon system development. The objective of PERT is the presentation of tasks, events, and activities in sequential form and in a network pattern, accompanied by estimates of the time required for completion of various parts of the network under different circumstances, and the identification of "critical paths" representing optimum grouping of tasks. Figure 5-1 shows a small portion of a PERT network analysis chart. The chief advantages that the use of PERT is intended to provide are the following:

Development of an intelligent, intelligible, and efficient plan
Accurate measurement of progress against the plan
Prognostication of completion of tasks and achievement of goals
Identification of potential problem areas before they actually occur
Capability to simulate and optimize plan changes and to determine impact of such changes upon program goals
Maximization of the effective use of resources

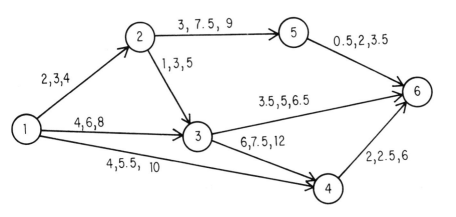

Fig. 5-1. Simplified PERT Chart. The chart shows numbered events, and three time estimates for each activity: optimistic, most likely, and pessimistic, respectively. Reproduced by permission from Joseph Horowitz, *Critical Path Scheduling* (New York: The Ronald Press Co., 1967).

In the case of the Polaris project, supervision was required for thousands of subcontracts (tasks) that had varying degrees of time-dependency relationships among each other. Their completion had to be monitored, and the tasks had to be so grouped as to permit the earliest completion of each of the program's segments. For that purpose, three time estimates (best, most likely, and worst) were made for each activity in the network. Using these as input, the computer then calculated the optimum critical path through the network, and applicable slack times. The principal outputs of the PERT system are reports showing event order, calendar time, and slack time. In its successful applications, PERT requires regular and frequent review of analysis by responsible managers, and constant updating and re-analysis.

As a result of the repeated use of PERT in both government and industry, it has been extended and modified in several ways. The most important of these extensions has been the inclusion of cost as well as time; this is known as PERT/COST. And because the technique of charting dependency relationships has itself served to increase understanding, many small businesses have utilized manually-operating versions of the technique quite successfully. But, large-scale applications would be quite impossible to manage without computer assistance.

Simulation is another planning tool in which the computer has figured prominently if not indispensably. Simulation combines pragmatic and theoretical techniques. Simulation (that is, imitation) is intended to test the effects, or outcomes, of various assumed situations without having to experience the real situations themselves. Perhaps the most colorful example is the military exercise of war gaming, in which military commanders and staff members test out various strategies without actually committing troops, supplying weapons, and so on at all. In fact, much of what has been learned of simulation has come from the military. In industry, computerized simulation models have been created and used for such problems as:

Inventory control
Plant layout
Job shop scheduling
Customer servicing
Warehouse layout
Warehouse siting and product distribution
Vehicular traffic
Marketing strategies

Fundamental in setting up a simulation experiment is the creating of a model to represent the activity being studied. This model must be based upon a breakdown of characteristic operating statistics, and usually employs algebraic expressions showing relationships of variables. A case history of model building is provided in a manufacturer's national distribution system, including factories, warehouses, and customers.[5] Various configurations of warehouses and mixing points were examined to seek what would provide the lowest cost pattern. The model included (1) customer characteristics, such as geographic location, order sizes and frequency, volume of purchases, and variety requirements; (2) factory characteristics, including geographic location, production capacities for each product line, and product mix; (3) warehouse characteristics, such as location, size, operating costs. Other factors, such as freight rates for all possible pairs of geographic shipping points, and effects of special promotion and pricing policies on customer ordering, were also incorporated. Various warehouse configurations were tested in the environment of customers and factories represented in the model, and the resulting effects on distribution costs were calculated. The computer output included for each factory, warehouse, and mixing point, a breakdown of costs, together with applicable shipment size classification and warehouse volume-by-product-line breakdown. Finally, recommendations for a national distribution system were generated, along with maps showing optimum warehouse locations and warehouse-to-customer assignments.

The technique of simulation—or better, the creation of a model, upon which the simulation depends—is one of a class of tools for solving practical problems known collectively as "operations research" (O.R.). Operations research is the application of scientific disciplines to solve operational problems. Among these disciplines, mathematical programming is used frequently in O.R. situations to help determine optimum distribution of limited resources, or recommend solutions when information is incomplete or subject to constraints. Mathematical programming has been used to solve a great variety of problems for both government and industry. It is, for instance, routinely used by manufacturers to determine product mix, including proportions and processes that will maximize profits or minimize costs when supplies of raw materials, machine tools, and so on, are limited. As

5 H. J. Heinz Company, described by H. N. Shycon and R. B. Maffei, "Simulation," in *New Decision-Making Tools for Managers,* ed. Bursk and Chapman (Cambridge, Mass.: Harvard University Press, 1963).

indicated in the preceding simulation example, optimum arrangements for factories, warehouses, and shipping procedures can be worked out. Another example is the determination of recommended alternatives among possible arrangements of machine tool capacity in a machine shop when the capacity for different machines is limited, and demands for different products vary. In some situations, the mathematical procedures can be applied manually. However, a computer is generally required, both because more general procedures can be applied and, also, because experienced operations analysts can be freed for other tasks.

There is obviously a great deal of overlap between operations and management planning, and computer and mathematical planning techniques can help top management decision making. Much of the record keeping and report preparation required for evaluation of current operations also provide the basic information on which management relies in preparing future plans. There has, therefore, been a trend in most organizations to standardize data so that, for example, reporting periods, units of work, definitions of terms, and so on, have uniform lengths and meanings. Information produced for a given task can thus find by-product uses for other applications, including enabling top management to monitor the pulse of current operations.

6

Computers and People

Some of the people who feel most strongly about computers must surely be those who have suddenly felt the impact of automation when used for law enforcement.

Take the case of the man from Cleveland, Ohio, who crossed the country to visit a crippled friend in San Bernardino, California. When the friend set out for the store in his wheelchair, the visitor borrowed another wheelchair and both were on their way, speeding down a steep hillside street. In their haste, they almost collided with a car driven by an officer from the sheriff's office, which wildly swerved to avoid them. When the officer angrily stopped and questioned them, the visitor's answers somehow aroused his suspicion—and so, he ran a routine check via his car radio through the FBI's computerized National Crime Information Center (NCIC) in Washington, D.C. Within seconds, the information came back that the Cleveland man's journey had been prompted by more than his desire to visit his friend, as he was wanted back east for armed bank robbery.

Also perhaps still pondering the interaction of man and computer is the driver in Buffalo, N.Y., who was stopped by a policeman when he inadvertently ran through a red light. Again as a routine matter, the officer requested a computer check on his car's license plate. The plate turned out to be stolen, but did not fit the car. So then the identification number on the car was checked, and it, too, was found to be stolen. In the back seat there were various items of office equipment, and a further check revealed that one piece of equipment was stolen. Suspicions aroused, the police obtained a warrant to search the driver's home. There they found: a 30-foot cabin cruiser, an 18-foot outboard motorboat, two 15-foot outboards, a 75-horse-power motor, several power mowers, numerous park benches and swings, tires and wheels, and auto accessories. In all, over $50,000 worth of stolen property was recovered.

Amusing as these stories may be, they also lead to some sobering implications. The inadvertent "heroes" fully deserved their misfortune. However, we may realize, and with somewhat ambivalent feelings, that we, too, are also affected. Whatever happens, whether we are guilty or innocent, whatever our age, sex, race, financial situation, or other condition, our lives will be lived against a background of computerized information systems exchanging with each other data that directly affect us, our families, and our property. True, we know that automation is a powerful factor for the betterment of our lives—and, in fact, that many things we take for granted today would not be possible without computers. However, we may frequently feel somewhat helpless as we experience the consequences of their unmatched efficiency or, occasionally, of their unexpected and always unnerving mistakes.

Computers, like all machines, have limitations. Therefore, to get the most productivity out of the costly devices, many organizations have altered their internal operating procedures, compelling their staffs, from managers down, to change the ways in which they work. And most of us tend to resent restrictions on our fancied freedom or spontaneity when we experience some "regimentation" in order to accommodate a computer's requirements. Also, we sometimes find ourselves caught up in what we may feel should be a responsibility of the data processing department—as, for example, when we are asked to fill out forms meticulously, letter by letter, in order to expedite the subsequent card-punching process. The unexpressed implication is that our failure to fill out the form correctly may affect the accuracy of a record, or even void it, and that the blame will be ours.

The growing tendency of large organizations to stereotype and standardize all references to individual people, by using numbers or other formatted name and address identifications, has caused a great deal of alarm to be expressed over the fancied or real loss of individuality. (Machines "like" to deal with fixed-length codes rather than varying size groups of letters, abbreviations, and uncommon spellings.) One noteworthy reaction to these objections has been that of IBM, the biggest single worldwide factor in the computer industry. It received so much criticism of its tendency to reduce human beings to a series of numbers that it has since restructured its filing procedures to process personnel by name.

The use of telephone recordings, computer form letters, and a multitude of other computerized activities in many business situations tends to diminish personal contacts and interactions. Where formerly one could write to people, speak with them, or meet them face to face, now one often deals only with a machine. Like urbanization, computer technology tends to isolate human beings from each other if they let it—an effect that man, as a social organism, finds difficult to tolerate.

Although speaking of social problems in general, Abbott Herman, over 20 years ago, summed up the situation that now confronts us in dealing with computers:

> Social problems arise, and existing problems are aggravated, when a society creates or accepts instruments of change, yet fails to understand, anticipate, or deal with the consequences of such action.[1]

NEW MEN FOR NEW TASKS

Many people fear that technological progress in general, and computers in particular, endanger their jobs. They fear that they will be replaced by machines that can do the work of many men. This fear is unjustified to the extent that the danger to the individual is far worse than mere technological obsolescence—it is "personal obsolescence." This peril is one from which even computer professionals are not immune. Computer technology continues to advance at a pace that quickly outstrips the knowledge of these computer professionals. Even if they were trained only a few years ago, they become personally obsolete.

The Harvard researcher and author Paul Armer has found that

---

[1] Abbott Herman, *An Approach to Social Problems* (Boston: Ginn & Co., 1949).

technological obsolescence of individuals is becoming a serious problem in technologically advanced societies. Alluding to the widely quoted "Peter principle," according to which individuals tend to rise to their level of incompetence, Professor Armer has postulated the "Paul principle," under which over a period of time, individuals often become incompetent at a level at which they once performed well, because they become uneducated (technologically obsolete) for that level. Borrowing a term from physics, Professor Armer has estimated that the "half-life" of a graduate computer scientist—the period at the end of which his knowledge will have lost at least half of its usefulness—is four years.

Personal obsolescence and the half-life problem apply to all areas where men work to make a living and advance their careers. Dr. Daniel Teichroew of the University of Michigan has studied management in an automation environment. Among his primary findings is that the most sought after university graduate in the United States today is one with a Master's degree in Business Administration (MBA), which includes computer science—because his education has the longest "half-life" among those of all management candidates.

Hiring young men whose skills have a slightly longer useful life than most is only a short-term way of avoiding the consequences foretold by Abbott Herman. Change, or automation, will remain a source of problems for organizations who neither understand nor cope with it. Computerization has changed the nature and support requirements of these organizations' operations, while making them more efficient. New management tasks have also been created in the process. If these new management tasks existed as formal executive positions today, they would bear such titles as data administrator, information security officer, or information control officer. When they are formalized in the future, the new management responsibilities they will carry will reflect the increased importance for the organization of information flow and control, and of management systems and related decision-making procedures. These new jobs have a lower-ranking precursor today in the person of the computer installation manager.

As his role is seen today, the computer installation manager holds a very unusual position in the corporate hierarchy. It is also a brand-new one—so new, in fact, that it has only really existed since the early 1960s, when the computer was already well on its way to gaining wide acceptance. This is so because the early computer installation mana gers generally were the company's former tab-room managers, low-ranking service department supervisors with limited education, slight technical knowledge, and poor managerial experience. They were perhaps the best, the only ones, to be had at that time. Yet, their recurrent mistakes and lack of imagination made many companies' conversion to computers or upgrading of current equipment nightmares of excess costs, lost time, and gross inefficiencies.

Today's computer executive must be a professional, thoroughly familiar with both the operation of computer installations and, even more important, with the nature and requirements of the applications that will be run on his equipment. In addition, he must have a high degree of management skill to maintain good working relationships with other company executives as well as with the people working under him. A good test of his competence is the soundness of his judgment in assessing the practicality of proposed new computer applications.

His role in the corporate hierarchy is an unusual one because he must deal with other managers in practically all areas of the organization. The importance of the computer support that he provides to their departments is such that he is perforce familiar with their activities and procedures. In some cases, the latter must be changed to adapt themselves more readily to computerization. These areas of interest are exceedingly diverse, including in their variety, bookkeeping and accounting, inventory control, periodic reports, management summaries, simulation, marketing projections and analyses, process control, information storage and retrieval, library and information dissemination, and mathematical researches. The manager must personally, or through his technicians, devise computer solutions to problems in all of these areas. He must also be aware of all new developments in hardware and software technology and operating methods so as to run his department with maximum efficiency and economy.

In some situations the installation manager may not be fully able to control the use of his equipment. This, for example, may be so that programmers not under his control can prepare programs ("open-shop" operation). This type of operation requires the establishment of additional controls to insure machine safeguards, standards for documentation, and priority arrangements, while still permitting free usage by the programmers. These considerations, and others that are strictly of an engineering nature, imply that organizational control of a computer installation that must serve a variety of departments should belong to a high-ranking corporate officer. This control should not be given to the head of a particular operating department, who would himself be a primary user of and competitor for computer services.

Considering how important a role the computer now plays in helping them fulfill their responsibilities, it has become important for higher level executives to be aware of the nature and capabilities of computers and computerized systems. These officers, department heads and up, through the vice-presidential level, should receive enough indoctrination so that they will be able to participate knowledgeably and usefully in discussions and planning sessions concerning computers and their usage. This indoctrination would also be, at least, equally useful to executives of organizations just starting to computerize or considering the use of outside or remote computer services.

The knowledgeable participation of executives is particularly important in the case of systems analysis projects. Whether done by the internal staff or by outside consultants, such studies frequently involve exhaustive, unflinching scrutiny of the basic premises on which the organization operates. Afterward, the recommendations of the study group must be discussed and evaluated. It is very important that high-level company officers participate actively in this process before decisions resulting from the study are made at the top executive level. Decisions that must be taken concerning computer matters are, if their effect on company operations or costs is sufficiently great, no longer technical, but business decisions.

THE LAST GOBLIN

A large part of the history of man's cultural development consists of the history of his superstitions and of the many unearthly creatures that dwell in them. But, over the centuries, witches and warlocks, elves and fairies, the elemental and nature spirits—all have dwindled away from our collective awareness and flitted like shadows into the realm of the cultural anthropologist. The last to depart have been the things "that go bump in the night," and in doing so give us an agreeable chill, or is it a thrill? Or, perhaps, we retained them so long because they fulfilled yet another purpose—an explanation of man's evil, or a reflection of his duality, or the ultimate scapegoats? Whatever the cause, man has given up his goblins with utmost reluctance.

Today, the computer seems to many to play the role of resident goblin in our lives. It may be our last goblin, but it probably is the most powerful. Also, it is certainly among us by our choice rather than by necessity. There are few subjects more popular than the discussion of how difficult man finds it to cope when confronted by the complexity of his own technology. Yet, there has been no period in his long history when man has been less helpless, in comparison to his ancestors. The extent to which his survival is assured as are his prospects of some education and freedom of opinion may well explain the glibness with which we berate our technology for enabling us to do so many things that our ancestors could not. Actually, technology is people. It is developed by people, implemented by people, and intended to serve people. This, therefore, also means that people, us, should control it—and it is possibly our failure to do so adequately that has led us to blame the computer even as we use it.

The ubiquitous credit card provides as good an example as any of how spotty our control of computer technology can sometimes be. It is unlikely that we could enjoy the convenience or the mobility that the card provides without having computers to handle monthly accounting for many millions of credit card transactions. We may, however, think of credit cards as something of a mixed blessing when we consider that we have no control over the security or accuracy of our personal and financial data stored in the credit card company's computer files. Similarly, we may have experienced the helpless fury that correspondence concerning payment of credit card bills occasionally arouses. This, for instance, occurs when there has been a computer error, and we receive a personal letter, actually prepared without human intervention or consideration, requesting payment of a bill that has already been paid.

There are many variations of computerized dunning for bills already paid. The payment will, under normal conditions, usually catch up with the computerized letter-writing process. The machine impulse that would otherwise initiate a second (third?) request for payment is then canceled. If, however, owing to human or machine errors, the record is not corrected, it is often difficult and time consuming to get the record back under control. The creditor (or the bill collector, or his agent) has too often made insufficient provision in his computer operations for checking errors or for system monitoring and correction. Variations of the story are common, and are the basis for much of the unfavorable publicity that has been bestowed upon computers. *Homo faber,* man the maker, makes everything, including himself, and, if the computer is a standard, his creations extend even to his own goblins.

HOW COMPUTERS FAIL

Most computer errors have human origins. However, machine-caused errors do arise in computer systems, even though they are lower than typical human error rates by factors of several thousands. Such errors are most likely to happen on communications lines when data entering or leaving the system is incorrectly transcribed. Even so, the average error rate is only about one character for every 10 million transmitted. Errors are sometimes also caused by the software provided for a newly installed machine by the computer manufacturer, which may require some modification to meet certain requirements. This is quite rare, and any such errors should be shaken out as they manifest themselves within the first year of the computer's operation.

Man-made errors include: *applications programming,* where the programmer made a mistake in writing the instructions for the computer to perform a specific task; *operator errors,* whose avoidance requires the establishment of checking procedures; *input errors,* when the information is incorrectly transcribed from its original form into one that computers can read; *system design,* when a system has been carefully and painstakingly elaborated, based on erroneous assumptions. All of these errors that are caused by men help emphasize how early is the stage of development that we have reached in the application of automatic techniques to the solution of essentially logical problems.

The use of computers for the processing of ever larger volumes of data repeatedly creates needs for man-versus-computer decisions. It must be determined which decision points must be resolved by built-in logic tests and which must be reserved for human judgment. Programmed or built-in logic also sometimes fails to provide for all conceivable logic situations or for necessary human interposition. However, society's needs and problems are now so great and complex that computers with steadily greater capabilities have become indispensable. And, when these capabilities have become available, new applications have been developed to create new needs for yet more computing power. We have thus become steadily more dependent on the computer for our survival.

THE THREAT TO PRIVACY

Knowledge is today the major force that fuels our society, supporting the progress of our technology and maintaining a relatively acceptable level of social order. Indeed, without an expanding supply of ever more detailed information, it is difficult to see how society could keep on growing, or even survive its own complexity. However, a hard-to-resolve conflict has been created in the process between "privacy" (information relating to ourselves, our families, and our property) and society's, or the government's, need to know (which often involves information relating to ourselves, our families, and our property).

The problem of privacy is not new, but where previously only a few wealthy or powerful individuals might have been affected, today it affects all of us. This, of course, is due to the efficiency with which information can be stored in computers and then easily retrieved in any desired format. This efficiency, however, is not always matched by that with which the stored information is kept secure from misappropriation and misuse. Thus, we have become all too aware that countless government and private agencies now keep records on us and that they are free to reveal them to whomever they choose, even if the effect may be to harm us without cause. This situation is largely caused by lack of proper controls, a human error. However, computers, the tools that made this possible, frequently serve as the targets of our protests, including the acid verses of Felicia Lamport:

Deprivacy

Although we feel unknown, ignored
　　As unrecorded blanks,
Take heart! Our vital selves are stored
　　In giant data banks,

Our childhoods and maturities
　　Efficiently compiled,
Our stocks and insecurities
　　All permanently filed,

Our tastes and our proclivities,
    In gross and in particular,
Our incomes, our activities
    Both extra—and curricular.

And such will be our happy state
    Until the day we die
When we'll be snatched up by the great
    Computer in the sky.[2]

An interesting historical footnote might be written concerning the ways in which technology has been used both to make communications faster and more confidential and to develop means with which to spy on the communicators and assault their privacy. Thus, telegraph tapping quickly followed the first widespread use of telegraphic communications in the 1850s. Similarly, telephone tapping accompanied, in the late 1880s, the invention of the telephone. In the next decade, the ubiquitous microphone was developed and promptly put to use as a means of hidden spying or surveillance. With its aid, the police and private organizations, such as the Pinkerton Detective Agency, made "dictaphone detection" a byword of the pre-World War I era.

Progress in gathering and storing personal information has, as we know, not stopped since World War I. Today, computers are used to handle the accumulation of vast quantities of personal data, some of which may be of questionable value to the prime mission of the information-gathering agency. The U.S. Army, for instance, collected information on the lawful political activities of many American citizens, including some well-known political figures, through much of the late 1960s. The FBI's files are bulging with similar information, as are those of the Passport Office and of many other government departments. A giant computerized central National Data Bank, storing detailed information from all government and many private sources on every inhabitant of the United States or visitor to the land, came close to becoming a reality in the late 1960s. A storm of protests and criticisms concerning the security and the ethics of such a data bank finally shelved the project, but it is likely to be resurrected.

While we may ultimately be able to exert some control over data

<hr>

[2] Copyright © 1970 by Felicia Lamport. Reprinted by permission of Cyrilly Abels, Literary Agent.

gathering by the government, we have no such control when this is done by private organizations—particularly if they happen to be our employers. Computerized personnel files are becoming common in many companies. Personnel managers value them because they believe that they help them select candidates with the best experience for specific positions. However, like any technician, they would like more data on the individuals and there may be a point beyond which their demands for information would violate our basic privacy, and then we might have little recourse against them. Also, the danger always exists that computerized selection can be programmed to meet other criteria—political, ethnic, and so on—than simply experience and efficiency.

Not surprisingly, publication of books and articles concerning computers and privacy is steadily increasing. Included among them are two studies in depth of the possible misuse of computers by governmental and other agencies, *The Assault on Privacy*[3] by Arthur R. Miller and *The Death of Privacy*[4] by Jerry M. Rosenberg. Both are recommended to readers of this book.[5] The possibilities that they outline of the subordination of man to the computer are sufficiently disturbing to emphasize the need for laws and regulations that will protect individual privacy and freedom.

Pope Pius XII said in 1958 that "just as it is illicit to appropriate another's goods or to make an attempt on his bodily integrity, so it is not permissible to enter into his inner domain against his will, whatever the technique or method used." The right to his own privacy is perhaps the last preserve of civilized life that man has a right to claim for himself.

PRIVACY: PROBLEM AREAS

Maintenance of credit bureau files and retail charge account bookkeeping were among the first major computer applications to be developed. They have also, from the very first, represented areas where our privacy was least protected and our reputations most vul-

3 (Ann Arbor: University of Michigan Press, 1971).

4 (New York: Random House, 1969).

5 See also Ashley Montagu, "The Annihilation of Privacy," *Saturday Review*, 31 March 1956; Alan Westin, *Privacy and Freedom* (New York: Atheneum Publishers, 1967); and Myron Brenton, *The Privacy Invaders* (New York: Coward-McCann, 1964).

nerable. Credit data represents some of the most sensitive information that can be obtained concerning an individual. It affects our personal life, our business life, and even sometimes becomes a consideration when we are applying for a position or must obtain a security clearance. How poor the security of this information can frequently be is indicated by Rosenberg. In his book, *The Death of Privacy*, referring to systems such as that of the Associated Credit Bureaus of America, he writes:

> The most disturbing feature is that credit bureaus, in contrast with federal agencies, are not regulated by the law. Instead, credit sellers mutually agree to keep data confidential by using a code number when requesting information. In addition to annual dues of $25 to $30, credit bureau members are charged fees by the parent organization for information on individuals.

The law has begun to catch up with some of the worst abuses. For instance, legislation was hurriedly passed in Massachusetts to prevent a bankrupt credit bureau's data bank, containing information on two million people, to be put up for sale to the highest bidder. Similarly, it is becoming possible for individuals to inspect their own credit reports and point out inaccuracies. However, until effective, and therefore costly, controls are stipulated by the law, credit bureaus will continue to represent a high-risk area for individual privacy.

Our privacy can sometimes even be endangered as a by-product of computer applications that are designed to make our lives easier and more pleasant. For instance, we can now, with a single phone call, access a computerized system and reserve a hotel room or a seat on an airline flight, rent a car, or purchase theater tickets. However, every time that we do so, our name and address is noted, and, all too often, this data may be misappropriated and included in one of the mailing lists through which our home and office wastebaskets are filled with unwanted and annoying junk mail. Even our telephone numbers may be thus added to computer listings of home numbers that are increasingly being used by telephone sales organizations.

An example of how widespread is the misappropriation of names for mailing lists, and how poorly these lists are checked, is provided by a letter that was received on Feb. 25, 1971, by the Washington (D.C.) Post Newspaper Company. The letter, which solicited a subscription to a nationally known periodical, was addressed to "Mr.

Washington Post, Stock Room." The body of the letter contained several carefully inserted, apparently personalized, references to Mr. Post by name.

The federal government was the principal backer of early computer development. Today, it ranks as the world's largest computer user, and the computerized files that its many agencies maintain on U.S. citizens are of a size to match. The Bureau of the Census is, of course, a major user of data that may often strike us as quite personal but that, legally, we have to supply every 10 years. Two other agencies, whose computer operations are of similar scope and have much more direct personal impact on individuals, are the Social Security Administration and the Internal Revenue Service. There are many other agencies, the extent and the security of whose computerized files affect us in some way. The latter aspect, that of security, is still generally unsatisfactory, even when great care is taken by the administering agency. For instance, the Internal Revenue Service is extremely scrupulous about maintaining the integrity of its information. However, this data is available on magnetic tapes to state taxation bodies whose standards of security are often lax.

Proposals for streamlining government operations through the establishment of a central data bank have aroused a great deal of discussion in recent years. The basic argument of the proponents is that the data bank's establishment would eliminate a lot of inefficiency and duplication, as many federal agencies often have legitimate requirements for the same or similar information. Applications of modern communications and computer technology would enable authorized agencies to have access to a central or regional store of data. This would make possible the generation of many studies and analyses that are not now available or feasible.

There are many technical, management, and political obstacles that would have to be overcome before the data bank project could be successfully implemented. For instance, different fields of knowledge and technology all have their own specialized terms and standards for expressing measurements and other observations. Subdivisions of the storage mechanism must reflect these. The development of formats and standards for technical purposes and also to control access to stored records would therefore be required for the successful operation of a national data center.

The very existence in government files of so much personal information, however, has, in recent years, caused concern that statutory safeguards of individual privacy may not be adequate. This concern was also greatly increased by the consideration of proposals by Congress for the establishment of a National Data Center. Most observers have stressed the need for additional legal safeguards to insure privacy and to protect individuals from harm through misuse. Among those testifying at the March 1971 hearings of Senator Sam Ervin's Senate Judiciary Subcommittee on Constitutional Rights, Jerome Wiesner, MIT president-elect, suggested creating a watchdog agency similar to, or part of, the General Accounting Office, to administer new congressional and judicial controls. Senator Charles Mathias, appearing before this subcommittee, commented upon the computerized files within the Department of Justice, such as the FBI National Crime Information Center on wanted persons, those on narcotics users and known professional check passers, the Organized Crime Intelligence System, files on offenders with federal penitentiary records, and records of the Immigration and Naturalization Service, as follows:

> While each of these data banks is currently separately maintained, the contents of each—with the exception of some intelligence data—is made available when needed not just within the Justice Department, but also to other federal agencies with even marginal law enforcement mandates, to state and local agencies, and in some cases to private establishments such as national banks. The federal stamp of course gives all such data the force and validity of gospel. Federal law, in fact, encourages the collection and exchange of criminal records under the aegis of law enforcement.

Senator Mathias also referred to Project SEARCH, the new 10-state data System for Electronic Analysis and Retrieval of Criminal Histories, which recently completed an 18-month demonstration period. He particularly praised its sensitivity to problems of individual privacy, amplified in the Project SEARCH Committee on Security and Privacy Technical Report No. 2. This report prescribes procedures for excluding unreliable material, continuously reevaluating included data, developing safeguards to protect information, and permitting individual citizens to see and check the accuracy of their own arrest records.

PRIVACY: ISSUES AND QUESTIONS

All beliefs and all institutions are being reexamined these days. They are being tested for assurances that their structure is still sound and their role well defined, that they are relevant to the needs of modern society and of the individual citizens that it comprises. This reexamination extends to the causes that we support—and the struggle for privacy in a computer environment is certainly one of them. However, do we know exactly for what aims we are now struggling?

At first sight, it would seem simple to define what we seek in the struggle for privacy. There have been so many leaks, so many abuses, that there should appear to be no doubt of what is needed. But, these are the aspects of life, the sloppy or the grossly dishonest, that can be relatively easily controlled once we are determined to apply proper controls and enforce them. What is needed is to determine just what is implied in the right to privacy?

The question of our right to privacy is all the more difficult to answer in that there is no definition in U.S. law of the personal information whose privacy we wish to preserve. The law contains no definition of information other than proprietary data, patents, records, and other documents required in business. And, if our right to the privacy of our personal information is not yet determined, neither is our right to public information. Should computer-accessible public information be accessible at no cost to all as a basic human right? Or should it be sold on a metered basis like utility services, or should public information services instead be supported by private enterprise?

Then again, another question, privacy for whom? Privacy for the individual certainly, but what about private and nonprofit organizations? As they become ever bigger and their power to affect us all rapidly increases, should they be required to disclose their merchandising or fund-raising data regularly so as to alert consumers? Similarly, political parties could be required to turn over their data and simulation models after the elections.

With respect to the individual, we may be beginning to discover that we will have to define human privacy better if we are going to have any. For one thing, we increasingly live in an environment where all things can be evaluated and measured. This may mean that the need for privacy will be reduced among children whom the educational systems of the future will train in order to see and evaluate their potentialities. Also, it is probable that what we now consider to be the limits of privacy will be pushed back in any struggle between privacy and public good or, at least, policy. In the process, we may have to redefine privacy and come to value the insights that can be gained from greater disclosure more than the security gained from concealing facts that often lose their stigma once they become public. The resulting strategy, whether it be one of privacy or of insight, will be a computer strategy.

7

How Computers Work

Computers differ widely from one another in their applications, costs, systems configurations, capabilities, and just about every other aspect. This diversity comes from the fact that computers are not single machines but systems combining central processing units, auxiliary or peripheral devices, systems and application software, and, not least of all, a great deal of human managerial experience.

But for all outward differences of the various computer systems or models, they all resemble each other exactly in the way they work. They are all organized into four principal functional units. They all use numbers in the same way to represent and to manipulate arithmetic and ideas, and they use the same basic symbols to express these numbers.

Finally, and most important, all but the very smallest computers with tiny storage capacities use stored programs. The stored program concept, introduced by Dr. John von Neumann in 1945, calls for the storage of all instructions in computer memory. Previously, instructions were stored in external media, such as cards or paper tapes, or were wired on plugboards, putting severe limitations on programming. The stored program concept is the most important single characteristic of modern general-purpose digital computers.

BINARY NOTATION

All computer operations are performed on discrete digits. We are all familiar with decimal digits, and the idea of using ten digits, 0 through 9. Expression of quantities greater than 9 requires the use of several digits together. This is called positional notation. For example,[1] a number such as 346 is read "three hundred forty-six." But, strictly speaking, we should say "three hundreds plus four tens plus six units" because it is the sum of three powers of ten, each multiplied by a number (coefficient) from 0 to 9; thus reading from right to left, 346 is:

$$6 \times 10^0 = 6 \times 1 \quad = \quad 6$$
$$4 \times 10^1 = 4 \times 10 \quad = \quad 40$$
$$3 \times 10^2 = 3 \times 100 = 300$$

$$\overline{346}$$

(hundreds) (tens) (ones)

Computers have been built that use decimal notation internally, but engineers have generally found it more economical, and simpler logically, to use binary, or two-valued, notation. Just as the decimal system utilizes ten digits in positional notation, binary notation expresses numbers using only two digits, 0 and 1. In binary expressions, a "1" or "0" in a certain position simply denotes the presence or absence, respectively, of the corresponding power of two. Using the preceding decimal example, the decimal number 346 would be represented as follows in binary notation: 101011010. As before, this can be shown as the sum of corresponding powers of 2 (starting from the right):

$$0 \times 2^0 = 0 \times 1 \quad = \quad 0 \quad (\text{units})$$
$$1 \times 2^1 = 1 \times 2 \quad = \quad 2 \quad (2\text{'s})$$
$$0 \times 2^2 = 0 \times 4 \quad = \quad 0 \quad (4\text{'s})$$
$$1 \times 2^3 = 1 \times 8 \quad = \quad 8 \quad (8\text{'s})$$
$$1 \times 2^4 = 1 \times 16 \quad = \quad 16 \quad (16\text{'s})$$
$$0 \times 2^5 = 0 \times 32 \quad = \quad 0 \quad (32\text{'s})$$
$$1 \times 2^6 = 1 \times 64 \quad = \quad 64 \quad (64\text{'s})$$
$$0 \times 2^7 = 0 \times 128 = \quad 0 \quad (128\text{'s})$$
$$1 \times 2^8 = 1 \times 256 = 256 \quad (256\text{'s})$$

$$\overline{346}$$

[1] This example uses whole numbers, but similar techniques can be used for fractional numbers.

Now, "101011010" may seem to be an awkward way of writing 346. However, mechanical representations of binary expressions are both natural and economical in engineering. For example, switches are either on or off (current flowing or not flowing); a voltage can be sensed as present or absent; a magnet is or is not energized; paper tape or cards may or may not contain a hole. All of these are physical embodiments of binary, or one-zero, representation. Each of the numbers in the binary number system: 0 or 1, is a binary digit, which is uniformly abbreviated into "bit." The bit is the basic unit of computer information.

The ability to reproduce and·express the most complex logic structures in binary form not only benefits the logical design engineer but is also of great significance for computer programmers. In their development of analytic flow charts for problem solving, programmers generally use binary logic choices at successive decision points. Binary notation is a vital factor in the design and use of computer hardware and software.

SYMBOLISM, CODING, LOGIC

The role of symbolism in computing is a fundamental one, corresponding to the role of the alphabet in languages. The computer is basically a device that "manipulates" symbols—symbols of numerical value, of mathematical processes, of logical relationships—and, through these manipulations, arrives at conclusions or value judgments that could not have been arrived at otherwise.

In computer programming, symbols or codes are used in several ways:

(1) as a group of bits to represent an alphabetic or numeric character

(2) as a larger group of bits to represent a numerical quantity

(3) as a group of bits, or one or more character codes, to represent one of a set of computer operations in an instruction

(4) as a fixed number of bits to represent a memory address in an instruction

(5) as any number of bits or characters, to represent any predefined idea or logical entity

CHARACTERS.   Using bits (ones and zeros) to represent an alphabetic or numeric character is similar to the Baudot system of 5-position or 7-position codes used in telecommunications, and in paper tape readers and punches. Although variations exist in codes used by different input media, once inserted, character representation in computer memory is standard within the particular manufacturer's family of equipment.[2] In computer applications involving streams or sets of characters, the bit group representing individual characters must retain these particular code identities during internal computer operations. Examples of such character representations are: individual and corporate names, titles, numeric or alphabetic and combinations of numeric and alphabetic designations for objects. Some common applications are: maintaining inventories; ordering, shipping, and accounting; alphabetizing lists of names and codes, and searching, updating, and publishing them. A set of characters that occupies a common storage location and is treated as a unit is known as a "word."

NUMERICAL QUANTITIES.   Actual computation is done in the accumulator register of the arithmetic and logic unit, and the numbers being processed are usually word-length binary expressions. Thus, in a computer whose basic memory storage unit is a 16-bit word (one bit for the algebraic sign and 15 bits for numerical value), arithmetic processes are performed on a 15-bit binary expression such as: 011011101101001.[3] Since the maximum value expressible in 15-binary digits is only 32,767, computer programs for such low capacity machines frequently include routines that perform double-precision or multiple-precision arithmetic processes—that is, routines for dealing with two or more words treated as a single number. Another common expedient for treating larger quantities is known as floating-point arithmetic. Most modern computers have such a feature built in, to deal with large-valued expressions without requiring undue attention by the programmer. In floating-point arithmetic, two words (or two parts of one word) express the fractional and whole number parts (mantissa and characteristic) of the logarithmic version of the number. Thus the number 14,185 in the preceding example can be expressed as 0.14185×10^5, and in the computer would appear as two

2 The American Standard Code for Information Interchange (ASCII) is an industry-wide effort to obtain standardization.

3 Decimal equivalent: 14,185.

words: the first word would contain the binary equivalent of 0.14185, and the second word would contain the number of binary shift positions (power of 2) required to bring the first to its true value.

OPERATION CODES. The computer instruction typically consists of two parts: an operation code and an address. The operation code is the group of bits (ones and zeros) that, when decoded by control circuits, uniquely defines a particular computer operation. For example, although the binary expression "000110" could represent the number 6, the same expression appearing in the operation code part of an instruction might correspond to the operation "multiply" for the computer's control unit, thus activating appropriate circuits in the arithmetic and logic unit for performance of the multiplication.

ADDRESSES. All information or instructions stored in computer memory has an "address." This is an identification, in the form of a number or label for the memory location where the data is stored. Thus, a complete 16-bit instruction might read:

> 0001100010111001, with 000110 representing the operation "Multiply," and 0010111001, the address "0185."

The significance to the computer would be that the number now stored in location 185 (decimal) is to be multiplied by the number in the multiplicand register (special storage for data about to be processed) previously sent there by another instruction, and the results held.

LOGIC CODES. These coding examples represent conventional or standard modes of computer operation. All modern computers also include capabilities for bit selection, and for shifting, substituting, and manipulating groups of bits within and among different words stored in computer memory. These features provide good programmers with a great deal of flexibility. By assigning arbitrary meanings to one or more bits, Boolean logic,[4] combined with the computer's speed, can solve complex logical problems that might be impossible to solve otherwise. The solution of logic design problems in computer construction provides a prime example of this. Similarly, simulations of

---

[4] After the English mathematician George Boole (1815-1864), who formulated algebraic processes for dealing with logic problems.

real-life relationships can be set up, and tentative solutions reached, using varying sets of problem parameters. Graphic displays of relationships can be plotted and mapped, using arrays of bits or characters and specialized, computer-controlled equipment, such as video display terminals or line plotters.

COMPUTER ANATOMY

All digital computers, regardless of make or difference in size and complexity, are organized in the same way—into four basic functional areas. These areas, which do not necessarily refer to separate units of equipment, are:

- Input-Output
- Control
- Memory
- Arithmetic and Logic Unit

This organization is portrayed in figure 7-1. Also shown is an

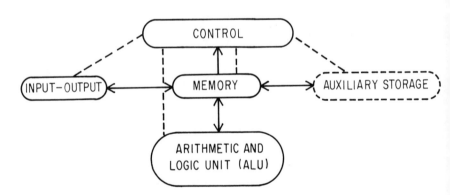

Fig. 7-1.   Computer Units

additional functional area, auxiliary storage, which represents an extension of memory. The solid lines and arrows in the diagram outline the flow of information (data, results, instructions, and so on). The broken lines represent control signals.

INPUT-OUTPUT.   The input and output sections maintain a two-way flow of information between the computer and men and other machines. Information and instruction of all types enter the computer at the input end. Computer output includes processed data and information summoned from computer storage. Both sections contain the logic to communicate with and control their respective devices. They also perform buffering functions to smooth over differences in speeds among the computer's various sections. The computer's internal operating speed, for instance, is so much greater than the slower rate at which information comes in through input devices that it would be very wasteful to slow the computer down to match input rates. Therefore, input information is "buffered," or stored, until there is enough accumulated for high-speed entry into the computer. Internal speeds are also much higher than those of output devices, and a reverse buffering operation is also required.

The bulk of the work done in most computer installations is batch processing of large amounts of information. This information usually comes as raw data—ledgers, documents, even handwritten notes—that has to be processed into a form that computers can use. The classical method has been first to keypunch the data into cards, and then to transcribe the information on the cards onto magnetic tape. An alternate method is that of transcribing the raw data directly onto tape, using special keyboard devices that are coming into wide use, particularly where the information is generally similar in format and comes in large volumes. State automobile license bureaus and taxing bodies are examples.

The magnetic tape used to store computer information is similar to that used in voice records, except that the tape is generally wider (½ inch instead of ¼ inch), and the recorded signal is in binary pulses (instead of continuous waves corresponding to sound vibrations). The chief advantages of tapes are their relative economy and the high speeds (several thousand characters per second) with which information can be "read" by the computer or "written" (transcribed) by it. Tapes are being rivaled by another medium, disk packs. These are packs of disks very much like LP records. The chief and telling difference is that disk packs permit *random access* retrieval of their information. This means that the computer goes directly to the location where needed information is stored on disk tracks, rather than having to start from the beginning of the disk pack, and having to read each of the several disks in the pack from the beginning until the information sought is reached. This time-consuming serial look-up is necessary with tape. Disk packs are also being increasingly used to store computer programs and other instructions, as these can be easily modified through random access. Previously, computer programs were generally punched into decks of cards for entry into computers.

Conversion of raw data into computer input is a troublesome part of computer operations because this is where the greatest numbers of errors can be made in transcription and not found out until the end of computer processing. This is in great part caused by the lack of attentive, well-motivated conversion equipment operators. Several methods for automatic conversion of source data into computer media are being explored. One is Optical Character Recognition (OCR), the automatic reading of printed or handwritten characters. This technology seems attractive, but its progress so far has been hindered by high costs and high error rates. The best results have been achieved when the variety of character styles and sizes was very limited, and the information to be read was highly formalized. Examples are the plastic credit cards that most of us carry. The account numbers printed on such cards are automatically scanned by character-sensing equipment to prepare computer input media.

Another method that has been successfully developed to the point where it is beginning to seem practical is *source data automation,* in which the very act of recording a transaction at the time and place it is carried out generates the automatic production of computer media. A prime example is that of the *point of sales* (POS) devices now coming into ever wider use in retail stores. POS equipment plays the roles of both cash register and data recorder, storing the information into computerlike storage, or on tape loops or cassettes. Some POS devices are directly on-line to a central computer. Another means of source data automation widely used in retail stores is that of attaching punched cards and tags to goods, particularly garments. When the goods are bought, the tags are detached and sent down to the data processing department where the data can be directly entered into a computer without any intermediate conversion.

Computer output information is generally transcribed into some machine media—punched cards, magnetic tape, or disks—to create a record for subsequent look-up. To be usable by human beings, however, this output data must be printed out as listings, reports, or whatever other format may be desired. This is usually done by "line printers" that print an entire line of 120 characters at a time at speeds approaching 2000 lines per minute. Faster speeds, which can exceed 5000 lines per minute, can be achieved by nonimpact devices using such techniques as electronic image projection combined with electrostatic printing. Their high cost, however, is seldom justified by volume. In addition, there are plotters, specialized machines that prepare graphs and other line drawings, using moving pens and paper controlled by computer output signals.

Printed copy can also be supplied by a console typewriter. This version of a standard electric typewriter is neither as fast nor as efficient as a line printer. However, it is used for that purpose with very small computers. It is useful with bigger computers to record diagnostic reports on system or program operations, comments or notices addressed to the operator-attendant, and intermediate or brief final results.

In addition to on-site devices, computer output may also be addressed to remote data terminals, located next door or thousands of miles away. Several hundred of these terminals, operating in a time-sharing mode, can access the same large computer at the same time. Typical time-sharing applications include theater, hotel, and airline reservation services; inventory and railroad car control; and many scientific, engineering, and defense uses. Terminals have become increasingly complex. For instance, the CRT or cathode ray tube terminal features a televisionlike visual display, with an input keyboard. Some are also equipped with light pens with which operators can "doodle" on the display screen, creating or altering images on the display screen. These "doodles," entered into computer memory, along with mathematical data, can be turned into finished designs, permitting the designers to evaluate their ideas, quickly dispensing with the need to build costly prototypes. This technique was used in the design of the giant C5A military transport aircraft. Two design teams, in London and Marietta, Georgia, shared the same computer, located in Marietta. However, the time difference allowed each team to use the computer while the other team was not working.

CONTROL. The control unit is not a separate device, but consists primarily of circuits located throughout the computer. However, it performs several vital functions, which include:

Decoding and interpreting the operation code and addresses in an instruction
Setting up the memory selection circuitry with which to obtain the number, or operand, at that address and directing its trans-

mission from Memory to the arithmetic and logic unit (ALU)
Signaling the ALU to activate the relevant operation circuitry

After the ALU has completed an operation, a signal to that effect
goes back to Control, which then resets the instruction address register and signals Memory to transmit to Control the instruction found
at that address, so that the instruction execution cycle can begin
again.

Other important control functions include:

Regulation of input and output operations, as in the case of time
sharing
Regulation of the computer interrupt mechanism on command,
or in case of emergencies
Responding to requests for operations status information

The capabilities of the control unit permit large computers to
operate in various modes, including *multiprocessing*—simultaneous
processing of data from several input sources—and *multiprogramming*
—the simultaneous running of several programs on a time-shared
basis.

ARITHMETIC AND LOGIC UNIT (ALU).   The ALU houses the electronic
circuits that perform most of the "work horse" operations of the computer program, following the directions of the control unit. The basic
functions that the ALU performs are the four basic arithmetical
operations: add, subtract, multiply, and divide. The ALU also includes a group of manipulatory instructions that facilitate the transfer
of complete words or parts of words from one Memory location to
another, and among bit locations in the same word. A third important
group of ALU instructions is that of the discriminate or "branch" instructions. The functions that they perform are those that seem most
like human thought in that they involve apparently conscious choices
between alternate courses.

Finally, the ALU includes special output instructions. These vary
greatly according to the scale and complexity of the computer in
which they are used. The simplest ones start or stop an input-output
device, such as a magnetic tape drive. In more sophisticated systems,
additional circuits allow simultaneous performance of internal computing and input-output functions.

MEMORY. Internal computer memory units store program instructions or data. Most are *fixed-word length* memories. They are subdivided into uniform length groups of bits, or *words*, the basic units for internal handling of data and instructions. One example is a small computer memory with a capacity of 1024 words. Each word, made up of 16 bits, is identified by its address, in this case a number between 0 and 1023. In a program instruction, each address is used to retrieve (read) the contents of its location, and to return (write) the information to Memory. During the retrieval process, the bits in the location are unaffected. Only a magnetic "carbon copy" of the contents is sent to control, the ALU, or output. The "writing" process, however, replaces or updates the original contents with new information. This memory operates in a random-access mode because the time required to access any storage location is the same as for any other.

The internal memory described here is also called main storage to indicate that it is at the top of a hierarchy of levels of memory, which, going downward, become progressively larger, cheaper, and slower. Typically, the memory consists of matrices of tiny (0.005 inches in diameter) rings or "cores" of magnetic ferrite material, strung at the junctions of intercrossing wires. Each core represents one bit of storage capacity. Thus, the 1024 × 16 bit memory used in the example would probably take the form of a stack of 16 matrices, each matrix being a square array of cores, 32 cores to a side.

Figure 7-2 is a simplified diagram of a matrix of magnetic core. Location of data stored in this matrix is accomplished through the grid of interwoven wires, with the presence of an electric pulse at the junction of a given row and column identifying the address being selected, much as we would find a street address. The diagonal wire senses the state of magnetization of the affected core. Each core can have two magnetic states, one corresponding to a binary "1," the other to "0." An additional inhibit (I) winding is usually required to inhibit, or prevent, interference due to overmagnetization. Related circuitry performs the "read" and "write" functions.

The cost of core memories has steadily declined, while speeds have risen. Modern core memories may be operated at speeds as high as 500 nanoseconds. Even these speeds are being eclipsed by those of memories made up of electronic semiconductors, which can be as fast as 100 nanoseconds. Semiconductors are now being used almost exclusively in "control" or "scratchpad" memories. This storage, while

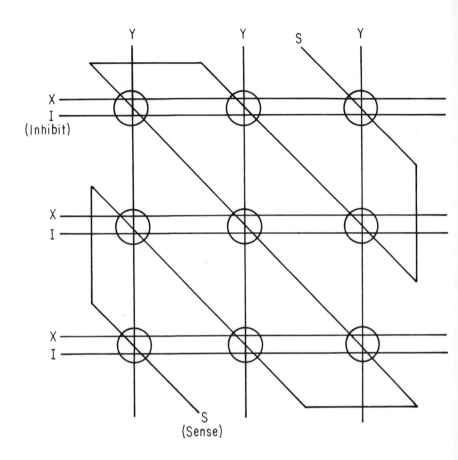

Fig. 7-2.   Simplified Diagram of Portion of Core Memory

limited in size, is much faster than main storage and holds signals, data, and instructions about to be processed, and that can thus be entered into the ALU faster than if they came from main storage. Semiconductors are also starting to be used in main storage, but core still holds a significant price advantage.

The availability of cheaper, bigger, and faster main storage units is important to the future of computing. The size of memories was restricted by costs in the past, and this, in turn, compelled the design of very complex software intended to minimize core storage requirements. In practice, this has caused high labor and operating costs and has been a major source of computer operating problems. In addition, new uses for computers, such as the creation of very large simulation models or extensive time-sharing networks will impose needs for substantially larger but economical main storage.

Below the main storage level, there are bulk and auxiliary storage. Bulk storage is a larger, slower extension of main storage. It, typically, consists of large core memories holding voluminous amounts of data in frequent use, or electromechanical storage such as large magnetic disks and drums whose economy is more important than their relatively slow access time. Auxiliary storage, or off-line storage, holds data that is used infrequently on disk packs, tapes, and other media that generally require human intervention to be entered into an input device before its information can be accessed.

PROGRAMMING

Lacking a program—a sequence of instructions as to what it must do, in what order, and under what circumstances—the computer is but an inert device that might as well not be plugged in. This utter dependence is one of the computer's most distinctive aspects. Most machines require some operating instructions, but the computer is the only device in which software is at least as important as hardware. In effect, the computer is really a hardware/software system.

Considering the fundamental role of programming in computing, it is important that we understand its basic principles—and, perhaps, it is best to begin by explaining what programming is not. Programming does not involve the definition of the analysis of the problem toward the solution of which the program is being written, nor does it involve the determination of the method of solution. These are vital steps in the program operation, but they are taken prior to the writing of the program, often without the participation of the programmer. In essence, programming is the writing of a set of instructions that will direct the computer to perform certain processing steps under given circumstances and produce certain types of results in a specified format.

There are four basic categories of instruction that are used in writing programs. These categories, which correspond roughly to the computer's four functional areas, are:

Data-handling instructions that are used to move data within the computer, bringing it from storage for processing or moving it to a given memory address.

Input-output instructions to control the external input and output devices that move data into and summon it out of memory.

Arithmetic instructions for performance of basic arithmetic operations. Included among them is the COMPARE instruction for computer determination of which of two numbers is the greater.

Control instructions whose consequences, like those of the computer's control section, appear to bear the greatest similarity to human thought processes. This appearance is caused by the computer's ability to "choose" one course as against another, following the criteria imposed by its control instructions. These instructions are also known as "branch" instructions because they call for a branching out of the sequence of program execution—around the next instruction in the sequence or to any other program instruction. Branching can be so ordered as to cause a set of instructions to be repeated over and over. This is known as "looping." Program loops are among the most important programming operations because they allow repetitive processing of similar sets of data, using the same initial instruction.

The computer's ability to make decisions comes from the conditional aspect of branch instructions. Under its program, the computer must either perform the next instruction in sequence or branch out. The course taken depends on the presence or absence of an "indicator," a criterion for action. This can include the presence or absence of a given number or symbol, a number being greater or smaller than another, and so on.

The different natures and uses of the basic computer instructions have supported the development of related programming techniques to speed and formalize the writing of parts of programs or entire programs. They include the following:

Loop processing for repetitive processing of new data or to modify addresses of data already in computer memory, until the unprocessed input is exhausted.

Tally processing, which is similar to loop processing save that the cut-off point is determined, not by exhaustion of input, but by the looping operation's having been performed an exact number of times, as indicated by a counter set up in computer memory for that purpose.

Address modification to permit easier access to data items stored in sequential memory addresses and to be successively processed in the same manner.

Search routines for location of specific information stored in a particular section of memory.

Sort routines for arrangement of various data items, such as numbers, in ascending or descending order.

Some or all of these techniques will be used in most data processing programs to make possible effective and accurate processing of data, using a minimum of computer time or memory locations.

The actual writing of a computer program is also called *coding* because the instructions are being coded into a form that the computer can understand. This is so because the computer has a "language" of its own, a code for internal conveyance of information. This is usually called "machine language."

Programs are seldom written in machine language nowadays. This would be too tedious because each of the many instructions would be a long string of numbers, consisting of a code number for the operation to be performed and another for the memory location where the data to be processed is stored. Originally, however, all of the early computer programs were written in machine language, and this was still being done in the Soviet Union well into the late 1960s. This is cited as one of the causes of the general backwardness of applied computing in eastern Europe.

The difficulties of machine language coding have been overcome through the development of assembly languages, symbolic languages that computers are programmed to translate into machine language. Thus, using an assembly language, programmers now write "source programs" that the computer, using a "translator" program, converts into a machine language "object program." The translator program is also called an "assembler." Some assembler programs are "macro-assemblers" that may translate individual source program instructions into several machine language instructions. These source program instructions are, not surprisingly, called "macroinstructions."

Several assembly languages have been developed that make use of macroinstructions. They are described as higher-level languages, and the assemblers that they use are called "compilers." These languages generally fall into either of two categories: procedure-oriented languages, or problem-oriented languages.

Procedure-oriented languages are, as their name implies, intended to speed and simplify the programming procedure. They are numerous because they have been developed for various types of specialized applications. Among the better known are COBOL (COmmon Business Oriented Language), long used for business applications; FORTRAN (FORmula TRANslation) and ALGOL (ALGOrithmic Language), both extensively used in the solution of mathematical and scientific problems; and PL-1 (Programming Language-1), developed by IBM for performance of both business and scientific applications on IBM System/360 computers. Inasmuch as the 360s and their 370 successors account for the bulk of all computers now installed, PL-1 has the potential of becoming the most widely used assembly language. It is also being adapted for use with other makes of computers.

Procedure-oriented languages are necessarily general in nature. Problem-oriented languages have therefore been developed to apply greater precision to the solution of specific problems. The GPSS (General-Purpose Simulator Language), for instance, is specifically designed to implement the creation of mathematical models with utmost ease, flexibility, and accuracy.

8

The Evolution of the Computer

Obsolescence is the theme that, paradoxically, keeps recurring throughout the history of computer development. The reason is a simple but momentous one. The development of computer technology has been so rapid that nearly all new computers are already obsolete at the time that they are built. This paradox has a long tradition behind it that begins with ENIAC, the first true computer.

When it was installed at the U.S. Army's Aberdeen Proving Grounds, ENIAC successfully passed its first tests. Its principal operations were performed in 20 accumulators, each 10 decimal digits long, in which the digits of each number were represented by the on-or-off state of one of ten electronic tubes. An array of function tables, amounting to 3,744 decimal digits, was set manually by switches to store constants. ENIAC did feature electronic circuits with which to perform arithmetic operations on numbers stored in the accumulators of function tables, and electronic control circuits for sequencing of successive operations. However, the operating steps or "instructions" were specified by manual interconnection of the various registers, using multicontact cables, plugs, and switches,[1] and input-output used

---

[1] Modifications were later made in ENIAC that corrected this, through addition of a limited amount of modern program storage, eliminating the requirement for manual interconnection.

IBM punched cards. Addition time was 200 microseconds, and multiplication of two ten-digit numbers took 2800 microseconds. Altogether, ENIAC contained about 18,000 electron tubes, and in spite of many pessimistic predictions based on estimates of average tube life, it performed surprisingly well.

However, even before ENIAC was completed, its designers realized that a better general-purpose computer could be built, with more extensive planning and better components and circuits. Mathematicians and engineers at the Moore School and at several other universities and research centers, including the Institute for Advanced Study at Princeton. Harvard University, M.I.T., the National Bureau of Standards, and the RCA Princeton Laboratories were already describing logical concepts of improved electronic computers and different approaches for constructing internal memories for such machines.

As the result of discussions among leading logical designers, two government agencies, the U.S. Army's Ordnance Department and the Navy's Office of Naval Research, agreed to cosponsor an eight-week course on computers in July and August 1946 at the Moore School. Just prior to the presentation of this course, in June 1946, Part I of the Institute for Advanced Study reports on "Logical Design of an Electronic Computing Instrument" by Arthur W. Burks, Herman H. Goldstine, and John von Neumann appeared. These reports and the lectures at the Moore School summer course together laid the foundation for the modern computer industry. Besides the three I.A.S. coauthors named above, others who made significant contributions to the course were George Stibitz, Irven Travis, John W. Mauchly, J. Presper Eckert, Jr., D. H. Lehmer, D. R. Hartree, C. B. Sheppard, H. H. Aiken, T. Kite Sharpless, and Hans Rademacher.

The Moore School summer course was attended by only 28 individuals, representing 20 government and private agencies. These lectures and the I.A.S. reports are important enough to deserve discussion because fundamental principles and procedures were described that decisively influenced future computer logical design, numerical methods, and computer engineering. The proposed I.A.S. computer logic, memory organization, programming methods, and internal arithmetic representation have survived in principle and underlie almost all present-day computers. Also, EDVAC, the Moore School's proposed successor to the ENIAC, with its multiaddress instruction logic and comparatively sophisticated set of instructions, was described by Dr. Eckert and Dr. Mauchly. Their lectures included the seeds of several sophisticated features that, while not all realized in EDVAC as finally completed, became commonplace in other computers years later. Automatic accumulation, instruction repetition, and indexing were among these powerful logic features.

Among other important contributors to the understanding of the new computing machines during these formative years, one who stands out was Professor Norbert Wiener, the author of *Cybernetics, or Control and Communication in the Animal and the Machine*.[2] In this, his most famous work, and other both highly technical and more general works, Professor Wiener laid the foundation for the philosophical linkage between old mechanistic and mathematical theories in science. A traditional concept of machines segregated them from the areas of reasoning; it was the exclusive province of "brain" to discover relationships, provide mathematical theories, and control the operation of muscles that in turn operated machines. The enlargement of the functions of machines to include more and more of what had traditionally been the exclusive province of the brain—so dramatically apparent in the modern computer—was recognized and explained by Professor Wiener. As Stephen Toulmin[3] says in summarizing Professor Wiener's contribution: "The essential step forward consisted in ignoring the whole of the traditional argument about mind and matter and in simply *doing* what mathematicians had previously assumed could not be done." If cybernetics did not directly contribute to actual machine developments or improvements, it did stimulate research in automatic devices and in efforts to explain and simulate human thinking processes.

THE EARLY COMPUTERS

During the two or three years after publication of the Institute for Advanced Study and Moore School reports, several computers were constructed in this country and in England. The roster of these early machines includes:

EDVAC   Moore School of Electrical Engineering, University of Pennsylvania, Philadelphia, Pa.

2 (Cambridge, Mass.: The M.I.T. Press, 1948).

3 Toulmin, "The Importance of Norbert Wiener," in *Perspectives on the Computer Revolution,* ed. Zenon W. Pylyshyn (Englewood Cliffs: Prentice-Hall, 1970).

SEAC	National Bureau of Standards, Washington, D.C.
SWAC	National Bureau of Standards, Institute for Numerical Analysis, UCLA
BINAC ⎫ UNIVAC ⎭	Electronic Control Company (later: Eckert-Mauchly Computer Corp., Sperry Rand Corp.)
RAYDAC	Raytheon Corporation
I.A.S.	Institute for Advanced Study, Princeton, N.J.
E.R.A. 1101	Engineering Research Associates (later: Division of Sperry Rand Corp.)
MARK III	Harvard University Computation Laboratory
WHIRLWIND	Massachusetts Institute of Technology Servomechanisms Laboratory
SSEC	International Business Machines Corporation
A.C.E.	National Physical Laboratories, Teddington, Middlesex, England
EDSAC	Cambridge University, Cambridge, England
"BABY"	Manchester University, Manchester, England

Of these early computers, the first two completed in this country (IBM's Selective Sequenced Electronic Calculator (SSEC) and Eckert-Mauchly's BINAC), in 1948 and 1950, respectively, were built primarily for demonstration and test purposes, and were not put to much practical use. Cambridge University's EDSAC was the first completed and was in regular operation by May 1949.

The earliest regularly operated electronic computer in this country was the Harvard Computation Laboratory's MARK III. However, it and its successor, MARK IV, were "one of a kind" and could be classified as dead-end branches on the computer evolutionary tree.

The National Bureau of Standards' SEAC began operation in the spring of 1950, at least two years before completion of EDVAC, its model. Many other computers were later built with logic based upon EDVAC design ideas. Also, the Institute for Advanced Study at Princeton had begun construction of an electronic computer, usually called simply the I.A.S. computer, along lines originally proposed in the 1946 report by Burks, Goldstine, and von Neumann. Although many delays made it one of the last of the pioneer computers to be completed (1952), many other computers were based upon its logical design ideas.

In December 1950 Engineering Research Associates (later a division of Sperry Rand) delivered to the Defense Department the first model of the computer that was later marketed under the type name E.R.A. 1101.

One of the most famous early machines, whose design was similar to that of the I.A.S. machine, was M.I.T.'s WHIRLWIND, which was started in 1947. The M.I.T. Servomechanisms Laboratory was responsible for many important developments, among them the first successful magnetic core memory, and several display and control techniques.

Then, in 1951, Eckert-Mauchly's UNIVAC I went into operation for the Bureau of the Census. Several copies of the first UNIVAC computer were bought by government and industry. With the UNIVAC I, computers ceased to be one-of-a-kind machines and came to be regarded as practical devices for nonmilitary applications. This operation later became a division of Sperry Rand; all of its computers now bear the UNIVAC name.

IBM's computer business really began with the introduction of the IBM "Defense Calculator," produced in limited numbers solely for Defense Department use. The first of the initial group of machines were delivered in 1953, and additional models were delivered under the type number 701. Following the tradition of the computer industry, the 701 was soon made obsolete by improved and more reliable models introduced by IBM and other computer manufacturers.

MEMORY DEVELOPMENTS

One of the innovations without which the modern computer could not have become a reality was the development of a way to store a large volume of data and instructions that was economical and fast enough for the solution of practical problems. The I.A.S. reports, as well as several lecturers at the Moore School summer course, discussed this problem at length. At the same time, several developers were actively working on the problem. These early computers used three principal types of internal memory:

acoustic delay line
magnetic drum
electrostatic storage tube

The acoustic delay line was developed around 1946 at the Moore
School by Eckert, Sheppard, and Sharpless during planning for
EDVAC. A succession of pulses (signal or no-signal) travels through
an acoustic medium, say mercury, from one end to the other of a
"delay line." (Figure 8-1 shows a diagrammatic view of a mercury
delay line.) At the input end of the line is a crystal that converts an
electrical pulse to a mechanical wave which travels through the
mercury to the other end, where another crystal reconverts it to an
electrical signal. The series of electrical signals is recirculated back
to input, after passing through detector, amplifier, and driver circuits to restore the shape and strength of the pulses. Also, in the part
of the cycle external to the delay line are input and output circuits
and "clock" pulses for synchronization. In mercury, the pulses travel
at the speed of sound, which is much slower than the speed of electrical signals, and thus the delay in going from one end of the line
to the other constitutes a form of storage.

In the EDVAC and SEAC computers, the mercury tank was a
glass tube about two feet long; the delay time was 384 microseconds,
or eight words of 48[4] bits at one-megacycle-per-second rate. Thus
the 512-word memory for SEAC was contained in one cabinet holding 64 mercury delay lines and associated electronics. In the UNI-
VAC computer, the mercury delay lines shared a common pool of
mercury, with corresponding input and output crystals mounted in
pairs at both ends of a large container. There were 50 delay lines of
20 words each, and the delay time was about 400 microseconds. Each
UNIVAC word consisted of 11 decimal digits plus sign; as instruction
word, there were two one-address instructions in each word. The
EDSAC, constructed at Cambridge University, under the supervision
of Dr. M. V. Wilkes, also used mercury delay lines working at 500
kilocycle rate. Here the access time to numbers was 576 microseconds; for instructions it was 288 microseconds. The memory could
hold 512 words, each containing 36 bits.

The magnetic drum represents another early type of computer
memory. Here the information is recorded by magnetizing (or not)

4 The actual computer word length was 45 bits, allowing a 3-microsecond interval
between words.

fixed positions on a rotating cylinder that has been coated with mag-
netizable material. A drum may be subdivided into lines, parallel
to the drum's axis, each line being identified by an address, and containing all the bits of a word. Thus, the number of lines around the
drum may correspond to the total number of words in the memory.
Read-write heads, placed at fixed positions corresponding to the
information channels and address channels, read or write information at the proper line when the address indicated in an instruction
is sensed at the address channel. The drum memory built by Engineering Research Associates for their E.R.A. 1101 could hold 16,384
24-bit words and had an average access time (one-half a drum revolution time) of 8.5 milliseconds (thousandths of a second). The early
computers that used magnetic drums as primary storage media
include:

E.R.A. 1101
MARK III (built at Harvard for the Naval Proving Ground,
Dahlgren)
Remington Rand's UNIVAC File Computer
Datatron
ALWAC-IIIE
Librascope Corporation's LGP-30
Bendix G-15
Burroughs' 220
IBM 650

Several other computers, which used higher-speed memories such
as ferrite cores or electrostatic storage tubes, also incorporated a
drum memory for auxiliary storage.

Because of the great variation in the early memory devices
between minimum access time (the least delay in availability of a
word, from memory for readout, or to memory for writing new information) and maximum access time (the longest delay in reading
or writing), efforts were made to minimize such delays. Minimum
access or "minimum latency" programming could improve the running time of a computer program many times, from fourfold to six-
fold for mercury delay memory computers to several hundredfold
improvement in the case of magnetic drum computers, over programming without attempts to minimize such access time. For example, in the SEAC-type of mercury delay line memory, all words

occupy some cycle position between 0 and 7 in tubes of mercury in which eight words are circulating. (See figure 8-1.)

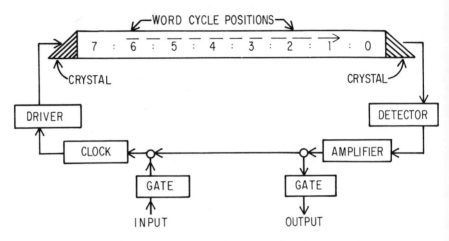

Fig. 8-1.   Mercury Delay Line (Diagrammatic)

Thus a word at cycle position 0 is said to be immediately available for readout and its access time is 48 microseconds (one word time); a word at position 7 would take 8 x 48, or 384 microseconds, to be read out (or written into). Therefore, instruction words and operands are carefully placed at memory locations that will be immediately available, if possible, bearing in mind cycle positions (the actual memory addresses modulo 8) and the known execution times of instructions. Of course, a major impediment to attaining ideal operating speed is the occurrence of conditional and unconditional jump instructions in a program. Even though the potential speed improvement in programming this type of computer is not very great, much ingenuity was lavished on programming large jobs, with often spectacular results.

In the case of magnetic drum computers, the effort expended was better justified because the potential gain through minimum latency programming was proportionally much greater. Here, as in mercury delay line computers, instruction words and operands could be strategically located, with due regard for instruction execution times. In the E.R.A. 1101 computer and possibly a few others, an engineering modification known as "interlace" was made to benefit from minimum latency programming. By varying the wired connections between the address selection register and the read-write heads, one could provide variations in distance between successive-numbered words stored on the drum. This permitted selective placement of instruction words and operands with less need for jump instructions. The interlace feature, at first implemented with a plugboard, was later made programmable. Minimum latency programming came to be quite an art, but the need for it disappeared with the advent of memories using magnetic cores, which were faster and cheaper, and which offered equally speedy access to all words.

The third early memory type was electrostatic tube storage. While planning for the I.A.S. computer, the RCA Laboratories at Princeton, under Dr. Jan Rajchman, was also developing a storage tube for computer memories, called the Selectron. The Selectron tube contained a number of discrete storing positions, or targets (256 per tube in the latest version), and a method of selection based on two wire matrices juxtaposed at right angles. Two adjacent wires in each matrix formed an electron lens or window through which electrons were permitted, by controlling voltages, to pass to the target, or selected storage element. The I.A.S. computer project, and the E.R.A. 1101, and perhaps other computers, originally had been planned to use Selectrons for their internal memory. Unfortunately, the project ended at the laboratory experiment stage, since the tubes were not reliable enough for computer use.

At about the same time, in England, Professor F. C. Williams was developing a computer memory that used a conventional television-type cathode ray tube (CRT). The Williams tube stored information on the face by focusing on the target spot. Such a target "hole" produced an electrical charge when scanned. Zero and one were differentiated by the presence or absence of a second hole. The storage method required periodic regeneration, about three times per second. The Williams tube storage method for computer memories was first successfully used in the "Baby," an experimental computer built in 1949 at Manchester University. A number of other computers built in the early 1950s used variations of the Williams tube for high speed memory, including M.I.T.'s WHIRLWIND, the UNIVAC Scientific 1103, and IBM's 701, 702, and 705. The access time for electrostatic tube storage was between 8 and 12 microseconds, but reliability was not nearly so great as that of magnetic core memories, which soon replaced CRT's in many installations.

Computers completed and delivered until 1954 have been characterized as the "first generation." All were quite large physically, and had large numbers of electron tubes. Because so many tubes gave off much heat, it was necessary to provide heat-dissipating equipment. First generation computers' primary storage mechanisms ranged from mercury delay lines and magnetic drums to electro- static tubes, and, finally, magnetic cores. The access times varied from a high of about 17 milliseconds to as little as 10 microseconds or even fewer. Contrasted with this memory speed improvement of the order of a thousandfold, internal circuitry speeds gained only a factor of two or three. Probably of most significance in the long run, computers attained much greater reliability, nearing the end of the first generation, helping to overcome objections from skeptics, cautious investors, and private industry. The "good operating time," or avail- ability in working order, of many early computers was as little as 35 to 50 percent, and they were "down" the remainder of the time. By 1955, machines were factory produced on an assembly-line basis, and were nearing 100 percent reliability.

THE NEW GENERATIONS

The invention of the transistor, virtually eliminating the need for electron tubes, and the perfection of production techniques, inaugu- rated the computer second generation (1958). Besides making pos- sible smaller and more reliable equipment assemblies and relaxed heat-dissipation, transistorized circuits soon attained higher and higher speeds. Also, magnetic core memories were becoming faster (around one-half microsecond access time), cheaper, and more reli- able. More powerful and compact computers soon appeared on the market and provided more computing power at a fast declining per- unit cost.

Another result of reduction in size and power requirements was the use, from 1958 on, of small computers in field applications, such as those in defense and in space. Indeed, in many situations, the cause- and-effect relationships were reversed; the impetus of space research drives and money hastened the perfecting of many of the required components and techniques.

A third generation of computers can be said to have come into be- ing about 1964. The first computers in this category generally used the recently perfected integrated circuits, or featured combinations of system logic improvements, miniaturization, and higher speeds. The introduction in 1964 of the System/360 computer family by IBM, the industry leader, is considered by many to mark the beginning of the third generation. IBM did not employ integrated circuits in the 360 series, but relied on a combination of small transistors with other solid-state components, which they referred to as "solid logic technology." Also, a key characteristic was the logical compatibility among all computers in the series. Other major U.S. manufacturers of third-generation, general-purpose computers are Honeywell Information Systems, Sperry Rand, Burroughs, NCR, and Control Data.

General-purpose computers are usually medium-scale machines. The growth rate of this segment of the computer industry has now been eclipsed by that of another subgroup of the industry concerned solely with very small computers, or "minicomputers." The leader in the minicomputer field is Digital Equipment Corporation, with its line of PDP computers. The availability and variety of minicomputers today spectacularly illustrates the tremendous strides made so quickly by the computer industry. In the fewer than 20 years since the first commercial electronic computer was marketed, it has become possible to build much more reliable machines about one-tenth the size and about ten times as powerful, for a hundredth of the original cost. Small computers can be used in modest-sized establishments or in several decentralized locations of larger organizations. They can also act as process-control devices having greater flexibility than special-purpose equipment, and as regulators, or "supervisors," for much larger computers.

SUPER-SCALE COMPUTERS

The term "supercomputer" originally applied only to a few extra-large-scale developments initiated to satisfy exceptionally heavy computation or data processing requirements in certain government agencies such as the Department of Defense or Atomic Energy Commission. The first computer in this category was NORC (Naval Ordnance Research Calculator), built for the U.S. Naval Weapons Laboratory by IBM. It was delivered in 1955 after about four years were spent in its design and construction. Its unusual design was the result of an extraordinary attempt to attain high-speed multiplication while retaining a basic decimal orientation. The high speed, for that time (31 microseconds for multiplication), was achieved by storing nine multiplication tables for the nine nonzero digits instead of conventional repeated additions. Although NORC did valuable work for many years, the device was not considered marketable, and no other computers of this design were built.

In 1955, about the time NORC was being installed, the Univac Division of the Sperry Rand Corporation was engaged with the Atomic Energy Commission's laboratory at Livermore, California, in constructing a powerful computer, to be known as LARC (for Livermore Atomic Research Computer). Its design proposed use of available components of known performance capabilities, such as surface barrier transistors, and magnetic core memory with four microsecond cycle time. LARC also proposed to obtain higher speeds by paralleling several computing units, and control of input-output by a programmed processor. The LARC fell somewhat short of promised performance, largely because of programming complexity. The first LARC was installed at Livermore in 1960, and another was built for the David Taylor Model Basin, near Washington, D.C. No other LARCs were built.

Meanwhile, IBM had begun work on project STRETCH; the goal was a computer 100 times more powerful than the IBM 704, then considered an industry standard. This would be accomplished by combining use of high-speed transistorized circuits, magnetic core memories having access time of two microseconds, and improved logic features designed to minimize "waste" computer operation time. To put these ideas to the test, IBM contracted with the two largest government users of computers, the Atomic Energy Commission and the Defense Department, to build the first two STRETCH computers. The AEC's particular interest was the higher multiply speeds; the Defense requirement placed greater emphasis on nonnumeric logical processes and on large-volume data handling. The final design solution provided the same basic STRETCH computer to fill the needs of both agencies and for other potential users. The Defense version included an additional attachment for special nonnumeric processing, and a small (2,048 words) higher-speed (0.75 microsecond) memory added to the 2-microsecond main memory, and also a specially designed magnetic tape processor of greater capacity and speed than any then commercially available.

The two completed machines, delivered in 1961 (AEC) and 1962 (Defense), fell somewhat short of the original speed goals, but have performed remarkably well in spite of some extraordinarily complex programming requirements. Another STRETCH machine, now designated IBM 7030, was delivered to the AEC's laboratory at Livermore, and six others were built and installed for other users. Because of the final lower speeds, IBM reduced the price from the original announced figure, and discontinued construction of the Type 7030. Although not commercially successful for IBM, the STRETCH research and computers resulting from it certainly "stretched" the state of the art, and probably provided the foundation for IBM's later third-generation series of machines.

Although both LARC and STRETCH did not become commercially profitable, it soon became apparent that a market for supercomputers did indeed exist, provided they could be dependably produced. In 1964, Control Data Corporation, a comparative newcomer but fast becoming one of IBM's most serious competitors in the very-large-computer field, delivered its first Model 6600 to the Livermore Atomic Energy Laboratories. This computer, several times more powerful than STRETCH, achieved this power partly from its use of multiple arithmetic and logic units, along with its ten peripheral processors. Still larger and more expensive computers were later offered by CDC: Models 6700 and, recently, the CDC Star. IBM's current offerings at this level of computer power are the System 360/85 and System 370/195. Among the other makers of superscale computers are Burroughs Corporation (Model 7700) and Honeywell Information Systems (Model 82).

Undoubtedly in a class by itself is the system under development at the University of Illinois, which is being constructed under contract by Burroughs—the ILLIAC IV. It will have 256 processing elements under the general supervisory control of a Burroughs 6500 computer. Because of the computer's unprecedented utilization of simultaneously operating parallel processors, ILLIAC IV designers predict that it will be faster than any existing supercomputers by factors in the hundreds. Of course, programming and controlling its operation will present problems of unprecedented complexity.

SPECIAL-PURPOSE SYSTEMS

Many computers, which were built to satisfy a great variety of specific functional and capacity requirements, have not been mentioned. In some very interesting developments, the noteworthy circumstance has been the creation of a *system* of operations, rather than specific hardware. For example, by joining new communications and display capabilities and the computer's inherent storage and retrieval powers with improved logical processes for regulating multiple-user access, some very powerful information systems have been created. Perhaps the first extensive system in this class is the SAGE early-warning system, developed for the Air Force's North American continental defense. Begun in the early 1950s, the first of 16 centers became operational in 1958. At each "direction center," a large computer system controls an elaborate complex of displays and communications equipment. Air Force personnel can instantaneously receive data from airborne early-warning aircraft, weather installations, picket ships, and other installations, as well as from other centers. The control programs provide for simultaneous access to system data by many users, stationed at consoles geographically dispersed and functionally different.

Other military systems have been developed, for different purposes, such as tactical data, logistical control, strategic command and control, and communications network regulation. The dominant function in all these is providing current information, and the outstanding current technological achievement that makes this possible is the perfecting of programs, procedures, and equipment for true on-line sharing of large data bases. This will characterize the coming of age of management information systems for nonmilitary use in the public and private sectors of society. Among the earliest large-scale non-military systems were those for airline reservations, banks, and the several stock exchanges. Law enforcement authorities have created nets of information exchange systems for use in apprehending fugitives, and, with the cooperation of the federal authorities, fingerprint and other identification information can be rapidly consulted and used to apprehend criminals speedily.

SOFTWARE DEVELOPMENTS

In addition to computer hardware developments, those affecting electronic circuitry and electromechanical devices, there is software, the other and equally important segment of the computer system. Software refers to the instructions that make the computer perform as intended, and to the systems and routines that maximize the efficiency and economy of this performance, and also make the programmer's job easier. The evolution of software has been quite as remarkable as that of hardware.

Of necessity, the first computers were programmed in complete detail; sometimes even individual bit patterns were laboriously specified when no shortcut had been developed. It was realized quite early that many programs, while differing in total objective and results, used shorter sets of instructions (subprograms, routines, subroutines) that were logically identical and interchangeable in different jobs or parts of the same job. As examples, instruction routines for solving certain classes of equations, for extracting roots, for arranging data within memory or for printout, for classifying and sorting, and many more had to be used and reused frequently for many purposes. Thus the idea of libraries of subroutines became urgent and economically necessary, to eliminate errors, minimize tedium, and minimize "reinvention of the wheel."

In the earliest significant steps toward software development, the computer itself assisted in program preparation. In "automatic programming," the computer provided, first, symbols or mnemonics as instruction names, and then, increasingly, other symbols as designations for more sophisticated capabilities. Thus, computer programs called "interpreters" transformed the mnemonics into actual binary codes that the computer could accept and execute. Other programs called "compilers" accepted symbols representing more complex operations, and compiled sets of such pretested routines. An important early activity that began to make such techniques pay off was the creation of groups of users of common equipment, to share their contributions toward the establishment of permanent subroutine libraries. The earliest pioneer in fostering establishment of such groups was Dr. Grace Hopper. The largest such group of computer users is the IBM "SHARE" organization. Similar groups have been founded by users of other large computers. The Association for Computing Machinery (ACM) also maintains libraries of subroutines and provides a communications medium for identification, publication, and exchange of algorithms and programs.

Many "languages" have been developed to transform the business of preparing computer programs from an extremely tedious and specialized occupation into a more universally available activity. One of the earliest was FLOWMATIC, a compiler language for the UNIVAC II developed in 1956 for commercial purposes. The most universally used compiler language was one of the first, FORTRAN (FORmula TRANslation), developed by IBM in 1957 for the IBM 704. FORTRAN has been modified several times for use in other computers.

To fill the need for a language particularly suited to data processing and business activities, the Defense Department-sponsored Committee on Data Systems Languages (CODASYL) in 1959 developed COBOL. (COmmon Business-Oriented Language). This has become a standard for most government users, through a U.S. requirement that commercial computers include COBOL compilers. Another important early language development was ALGOL, specially suited for algebraically expressed requirements.

Literally hundreds of other, more specialized, applications languages have been created. Their functions include those of executives, who supervise running of other programs; data managers and editors; error detectors; time-sharing supervisors; display aids; and others. A few of the better-known special-purpose languages are:

Computer Language	Purpose
FLOWMATIC	compiler for commercial users
FORTRAN	FORmula TRANslator; scientific uses
ALGOL	Algebraic translator; mathematical uses
COBOL	commercial data processing compiler
SNOBOL	language translation; program compilation; combinatorial problems
BASIC	time-sharing programming languages
APT	automatic control of machine tools
JOVIAL	military applications
LISP	list processor
GPSS	general purpose system simulator
SIMSCRIPT	simulation language
PL/1	combined scientific, algebraic, and commercial use

PAST, PRESENT, AND FUTURE

Computers have steadily become faster and more powerful, and will continue to do so in the future as they have done in the past and are doing today. However, computers operate in a human environment—and hardware and software innovations without human support are unusable.

On completion of Harvard's MARK IV computer in 1951, Howard H. Aiken expressed his belief that computer speeds were far ahead of man's ability actually to use computers. He recommended that man devote his energies to learning how to program and use computers already in existence instead of building bigger and faster machines. Probably, no one took seriously Dr. Aiken's recommendation to stop engineering research and development. However, his recognition of the need to understand better how to use computers was sound, and now, 20 years later, it still remains good advice. Much of the blame that is put on computers is actually because of poor planning, weak system preparation, and other human errors. Better preparation for using computers and better understanding of the computer by its managers can aptly be called "prescriptions for survival."

9

Solving Computer and Human Problems

Behind the squirrel's caching nuts, the dog's burying bones, or even our visit to a fortune-teller, lies a powerful drive to prepare for the future and what it may bring. Man has always yearned to eliminate uncertainty from his destiny. Farmers would obviously like to base their future plans on foolproof knowledge of what the weather will be for the next growing season. And, just think of the power that would accrue to any fashion designer able to predict accurately the public reaction to particular styles! And what about economists, politicians, and gamblers? All of them (with the obvious exception of squirrels and dogs), all of us, now believe, or have been led to believe, that an answer to our problems will in time come from the computer.

Enthusiastic claims that "computers can do anything" have now become clichés. Some people even seem to look upon the computer as "an answer in search of a question." Yet, simply because a job can be done does not mean that it should be done. Computers, too, have problems—not just those that they solve. Some are basic questions of economics and machine operation, but others are of such magnitude that they may affect our entire society.

COMPUTER PROBLEMS

In theory, a suitably equipped computer can do anything, but that is just theory. There are at least six very practical considerations for which satisfactory answers should be forthcoming before the decision is taken to run any particular application on a computer. These considerations fall under the following six headings:

1. *Definition*—is the problem-solving procedure completely understood?
2. *Repetitiveness*—is the program likely to be used again and again?
3. *Data availability*—is needed input information clearly defined and is it available?
4. *Balance*—what is the relationship between the input, computation, and output work loads, and are disproportionate demands being imposed on any one segment of the processing cycle?
5. *Economics*—is the job economically feasible when carried out with the existing equipment and staff?
6. *Public policy*—is the objective of the program a lawful one? And, if it is legal, is it "fair" and equitable? Are there any technical safeguards against misuse?

DEFINITION.   What we call a program is actually a complex procedural package whose effectiveness is only as strong as the logic underlying each of its steps and elements. Every possible consideration must have been foreseen and planned for in advance—and this includes any variations in the values represented in the data, the numerical sums and results arrived at during the computing process, and the form and contents of the final output results. A logic flow chart can be an indispensable aid in this process.

When a possible computer application is to be defined, the most important question that must be asked and answered is that of whether the proposed problem-solving procedure is completely logical, thus certain to yield the desired results. The individual elements of such a procedure must therefore be known before it is submitted for evaluation. In many, perhaps most, cases, the algorithm that stands for the most suitable machine procedure represents a far different approach from the one that a human being would follow. Yet, it must be logically demonstrable that the procedure will actually work. There have been far too many instances of sophisticated programs malfunctioning after they had been used for a year or more and were assumed to have been completely "debugged" (checked out for logic and programming correctness). The remaining logic errors were revealed through the input of particular combinations of data whose use had not been foreseen in writing the program. Thus, logic faults remained after debugging because the test data used could not reflect some of the almost unlimited variations of possible inputs.

Occasionally, there are computer applications whose objectives cannot be strictly defined. One example is that of a program to generate music or new art forms from essentially random input. Here, the definition must take the form of statements of transformation together with the rules for selection. Acceptability of the product will depend upon adherence to these rules rather than on a selective evaluation of the resulting "art form." Another type of program whose logic is difficult to prove is found in the class of "self-adaptive" jobs. Certain basic statistical analyses have been perfected through which the program objective itself is developed and adjusted in the course of the analyses. Yet, even here, the modular nature of the group of routines that compose the whole makes it easier to check out the correctness and completeness of the logic of the program.

REPETITIVENESS. The process of writing a program, creating and coding a practical problem for a computer, is usually both painstaking and time consuming. A program's reusability is therefore an obvious advantage. For instance, a payroll program will be used over and over again, and, if it has been carefully planned, it should be easily adaptable to any but the most basic changes in payroll procedures. This emphasis on reusability should extend even to "one-time" programs written at management insistence for high-priority applications—and efforts should be made to include in such programs features that would make them reusable with a minimum of adaptation. In this way, the computer's human support (the programmer) can be used to best advantage.

DATA AVAILABILITY. Whatever powers computers possess, they cannot be used without adequate input information—and it is this problem of data availability that has prevented some of the most potentially beneficial uses of computers. For example, it has been claimed that enough is known about the workings of the weather for accurate weather forecasts to be prepared, using computers to solve the many simultaneous equations needed to represent "all" variables affecting the weather. Perhaps this is true, though there are many who state that we do not have even a fraction of the needed knowledge, but we are as yet physically unable to obtain readings for the fantastically large number of variables that enter into the process.

There are many other examples of jobs not being performed because data is too costly to obtain or measurements too difficult to make. Sometimes the only obstacle is that of different groups of people disagreeing about definitions of terms and standard measurements. For instance, the use of computers to process and retrieve information has lagged in the fields of documentation and library services, largely because of data definition difficulties. These difficulties are mainly those of finding consistent meanings and bibliographic term definitions within linguistic frameworks. There are similar lags in other fields, and powerful mathematical and statistical tools that could aid long-range planning by business and government often go unused because of a lack of data.

BALANCE. The justification of a proposed computer job depends largely on how efficiently it can be performed, using available facilities. One method for evaluation of this efficiency is to consider every job as having three segments: input, computation, and output. If the processing requirements for any of these segments are described as either large (L) or small (S), then any job can be characterized as belonging to one of eight possible classes, as shown in the diagram below:

Job Class

		0	1	2	3	4	5	6	7
	Input	S	S	S	S	L	L	L	L
SEGMENT	Computation	S	S	L	L	S	L	S	L
	Output	S	L	S	L	S	S	L	L

The question of balance also affects the initial selection of equipment for a computer installation. Thus, an installation whose work load consisted mainly of mathematical computations based on relatively scant and infrequent data input could not justify the cost of high-speed input devices or large-capacity printers. If most of the jobs at such an installation were Class 2 jobs (Small, Large, Small), this would represent efficient and well-balanced use of the available equipment. The Class 0 problem does not justify an on-site computer installation, but it can be handled by a central system, using remote batch or time sharing.

The characteristics of Class 6 are those of most business data processing jobs that involve updating of large files. Classes 6 and 7 typify the true data processing problems in which information flow in and out are of the same order of magnitude. The operations most frequently performed there would be file maintenance, sorting, collating, extracting, and so on. Generally, situations where different equipment is being used at uneven rates should be considered unbalanced. In considering the desirability of a proposed program, the analyst must prepare rough time estimates of each of the three processing segments.

ECONOMICS. When a new computer application is planned, there is a logical question to be answered, which, surprisingly, often goes unasked: "Is the job actually worth doing on a computer?" There are many tasks that would be uneconomical to perform on a computer or on a certain computer equipment configuration. In the latter case, it would be obviously wasteful to use a small-scale, scientifically oriented installation whose only output device might be an electric typewriter to produce large quantities of printout sheets or address labels.

The responsibility of determining whether a given job is economically feasible belongs to the programmer or analyst. This is not a matter of just making a flat "yes" or "no" judgment, but also of seeing whether the job can be done after all, even though it may seem prohibitive at first. For example, in the case of an installation with limited magnetic tape flexibility, it is sometimes possible to subdivide the total effort, generate tables of partial answers, and run a small portion at a time for table look-up, recombination, and output. However, even if the job can somehow be done, it may still be unwise to do it and so perpetuate uneconomical equipment utilization.

The economics of particular computer jobs can be analyzed in objective terms, so as to enable one to decide whether or not they should be done on a computer. The total cost of running a problem on a computer may be expressed as the sum of the following:

> *Programming cost* (programmer salaries × estimated programming time)
>
> +
>
> *Debugging cost* (cost of machine time + cost of programmer's time)
>
> +
>
> *Data preparation cost* (number of times different data are required × cost of editing, punching, and checking)
>
> +
>
> *Operating cost* (expected number of times problem will be run × machine cost per run)

The cost of running the problem one time can be separately calculated wherever applicable. However, the effective cost per run obviously decreases as the number of times the program is used increases. Also, the estimate of programming cost can represent a complex trade-off of the advantages and disadvantages of different programming approaches. Differences in equipment configurations (larger memory, auxiliary disk or drum storage, off-line conversion devices, and so on) can be reflected in both the programming logic and the speed of machine operations. Thus, for really large-scale applications, it may actually be more economical in the long run to modify the existing equipment installation.

PUBLIC POLICY.   All the considerations that have been discussed in this chapter have been of primary concern to the analyst or programmer. There are also questions relating to public policy, legality, and morality that will require decisions by higher-level, nontechnical management. However, technical personnel will often be the first to become aware of possible improprieties and other situations that will require management attention.

An example of what may occur is the possible requirement to use one or more tables of physical (or other) constants in order to perform some calculation. However, these tables must be copied from copyrighted reference works and stored on computer tapes or in memory. Permission of the copyright owner may be required, particularly if the output, including the tables, is to be printed and disseminated.

Another example concerns the protection of personal and confidential information about individuals obtained in the course of routine credit investigations. The relevant provisions of the law should be known and understood by all those exercising responsibility in situations where invasions of privacy may occur.

There are several pertinent questions that must be asked about the privacy and security of any system that stores information about individuals. Does the system include effective safeguards against unauthorized use of private information? Does it provide methods for personal identification to limit and control access to stored data? Are there arrangements for keeping stored information up to date, including disposal of civil and criminal suits? Can the affected individuals inspect their own records and react to or correct any errors? Is the system purged at reasonable intervals? Questions of this nature have been considered and incorporated by Paul Baran[1] in the following suggestions of how to protect information in large data centers:

Provide minimum cryptosecurity
Never store data "in clear"
Provide for random audit of use of file-manipulating programs
Observe careful ground rules applying to access rights in cross-system interrogation
Design built-in mechanisms to detect abnormal system use
Build into the system automatic checks, records, and authentication of information requests
Perform audits and reports of misuse

COMPUTERS AND PROBLEM-SOLVING TECHNIQUES

Computer problems are those experienced in setting the machines to work on and solve our own human problems. The importance of these computer problems will continue to grow as our dependence on computers increases. Through them we are becoming better able to fulfill one of mankind's deepest desires—to be able to visualize our future, and not only as the result of natural law but as a consequence of chance as well.

Natural phenomena are predictable to a certain extent—as, for

[1] Cited in Robert O. MacBride, *The Automated State* (Philadelphia: Chilton Co.—Book Division, 1967).

example, the motion of planets, the changes of seasons, the behavior of some species of animals. However, in most decision-making situations, we are usually confronted by a complex interaction among human beings, coinciding with natural phenomena. In effect, for each person in a "system" of actions and reactions, his own action in given situations is influenced by his appraisal of the action. That action then, in turn, itself becomes a factor affecting the appraisals and behaviors of all others in the system. A poker game is a system, in which each player's action is based not only on a set of knowns (his hand and other players' open cards) and unknowns (other players' hands), but also on all players' actions and reactions to each other.

In the real-life situations in which we are involved, we can use current and old information to decide future actions. We must use any observations and measurements that might affect the outcome. We are likely to temper our decisions by observation of trends that may be apparent in old and current data. For example, the stock market speculator plots the recent behavior of particular securities so as to predict their future price trends. Other factors—political, labor relations, import or export regulations, and so on—may influence the speculator's decision on whether to buy, sell, or hold a certain stock. Every time that he makes or "computes" a decision, the same speculator is actually solving an equation of overwhelming complexity. This complexity is caused both by the diversity of the data and the difficulty of gathering it (of knowing what to measure as well as how to measure it), and by the difficulty of expressing the interaction among all the factors (complex and usually nonlinear relationships).

Computers are obviously useful in solving complex problems which incorporate a great variety of data. However, their efficiency is no greater than the reliability of their input information. For instance, it is difficult to use them to help answer the question of how to cope best with the problem of drug addiction. Information on users, pushers, and the factors affecting the drug supply, for instance, is generally unreliable. Similarly, many new products or technologies are being developed without concern being given to their possible effect on the environment because the relevant factors are either unknown or hard to identify. Computers, in such cases, would have been only of very limited use, if they had not found their true role in the support of and increasing the effectiveness of a fundamental problem-solving technique—systems analysis.

Systems analysis is sometimes referred to as a new science. Actually, systems science was practiced by most of the classic scientific thinkers, beginning probably with Isaac Newton. The development of systems methods advanced dramatically in the 20th century as a result of their use in World War II. This led to the development of radar, advanced feedback control systems, and even the electronic digital computer. Scientific applications of sophisticated mathematical methods to simulation of military operations, sometimes called "war gaming," laid the foundation for the new science of Operations Research (OR), which is defined below:

> . . . the use of analytic methods adopted from mathematics for solving operational problems. The objective is to provide management with a more logical basis for making sound predictions and decisions. Among the common scientific techniques used in operations research are the following: linear programming, probability theory, information theory, game theory, Monte Carlo method, and queuing theory.[2]

OR combines techniques from mathematics, economics, and statistics to help solve dynamic problems in situations of conflict, complexity, or uncertainty. According to Sippl, the typical steps in an OR study are as follows:

1. Definition and statement of the problem and its components.
2. Correlation of all relevant data and reduction to principal variables.
3. Construction of model representing quantitative relationships of principal variables.
4. Check of validity and reliability of the model structure and decision rule.
5. Manipulation of the model to estimate, predict, and project the solution values under varying circumstances.
6. Selection of the optimum course of action based on predetermined decision criteria.
7. Continuing checks on validity and variations of the model with changing parameter values.[3]

Use of computers in OR represented the real beginning of practical OR applications. Various assumptions can be tested by creating

[2] Charles J. Sippl, *Computer Dictionary and Handbook* (Indianapolis: Howard W. Sams & Co., 1966).

[3] Sippl, *Computer Dictionary and Handbook*.

a computerized version of the model of an activity. Sets of data values allow the computer to carry out the operations indicated by the model, and derive resulting implications. Simulation of complex situations, by computer, thus enables management to test alternative possible courses of action without taking excessive risks.

Operations research techniques are useful only if their limitations are fully appreciated. Thus, everything depends on the completeness with which the relationships between the variables are expressed, and the taking into account of all factors that affect the outcome.

The story is told of a business executive who employed an OR consultant to advise him on major management decision alternatives. The consultant studied the business and all of its operations and records. He then submitted his recommendations, including a suggestion that one particularly incompetent employee be fired. "Oh no, we can't fire him!" cried the executive, "He's my brother-in-law!" The consultant had obviously overlooked one essential fact in his study.

THE OPERATIONS RESEARCH PROCESS

Out of the seven basic steps in an OR study, the first two represent what may be called the "systems analysis" phase, because the "systems approach" is used in carrying them out, following the definition below:

> ... looking at the overall situation rather than the narrow implications of the task at hand: particularly, looking for interrelationships between the task at hand and other functions which relate to it.[4]

Systems analysis may seem like the most obvious, the common-sense approach, but it also turns out to be exceedingly difficult to execute. At every management level, even the very lowest, there is some element of planning—planning the day's work, for instance, of the steps with which to carry out a task. However, nearly all operations affect others than the planner alone, and their planning therefore entails the consideration of influences outside one's control. For example, government regulations affecting licensing, minimum wages, and taxes must be understood and provided for in a business under-

---

[4] Sippl, *Computer Dictionary and Handbook.*

taking. The higher the level of planning, the more significant the systems approach becomes. At the higher planning levels, the factors to be considered include not only those affecting the present task but also those that are likely to require active consideration in the future. Therefore, it is essential to estimate the effects of projects being planned on other developments, events, and attitudes, and, similarly, the effect of others' projects upon our own plans, developments, and attitudes.

Mathematical modeling, the third OR step, has been used in many types of business applications, including:

production and inventory control
shipping and scheduling in warehousing operations
sales and marketing strategy
product mix
factory process control
lowest cost production
capital investments
meeting product specifications
optimization in price-cost-sales relations

Among the techniques suitable for these applications, the analyst may use probability and statistics, game theory, various ways of calculating maximums and minima, sampling, simulation, linear and dynamic programming, factor analysis, and simulation. Some of these are more rigorous than others; that is, the technique is relatively self-contained and will yield a solution. Those that must allow for uncertainty, or must choose among alternatives without control of some of the factors affecting the decision, may use trial-and-error in repeated simulations of the operation under different conditions. This means that the analyst must obtain the best possible information, perceive the distinctions in degrees of reliability of estimates, and include suitable allowances for such reliability variation in preparing models.

Mathematical models have many advantages when used in management situations. They are useful as succinct expressions of quantitative relationships among the factors affecting a situation. They help pinpoint what data need to be collected, and establish measures of effectiveness. They also enable one to understand and deal with all major variables of a problem simultaneously. All this is done through the use of computers, which make it possible to obtain solutions that could not be practically sought otherwise. The basic form of the mathematical model is usually a set of equations that express interactions among the variables. The activities of most businesses or other large organizations can be described by one or more of the following[5] types of equations:

1. Definitional equations
2. Technological equations
3. Behavioral equations
4. Institutional equations

Definitional equations deal with the principal basic operating facts of business life, such as profits, sales, costs, and breakdowns of these into their components. Technological equations express the physical processes underlying operating situations, for example, the mix of raw materials, plant labor, and equipment to produce goods. Behavioral equations include human behavior as a component, and are therefore less precise. Provision should be made to show, if necessary, a wide allowance for random error. Institutional equations must provide for external constraints affecting a business, such as the effects of the locality in which a plant is situated, government tax problems and policies, bank lending policies, and industry and trade practices.

Of course, the four types of equations may be combined in various ways, to test interaction of the different factors in a number of assumed configurations. And in making various assumptions as to alternative situations, for purposes of planning ahead, the equations may be manipulated, in effect, backward; that is, a desired output result may be postulated and the input parameters calculated, whether they be technological, institutional, behavioral, or definitional types, or combinations. The equations may, in some cases, reflect behavior among the variables that is not a linear relationship; that is, the change of one quantity as a consequence of another change may not be a proportional or straight-line relation. Such relationships will require the use of equations that are quadratic or higher order; constantly changing relationships may suggest the use of calculus to depict limits and trends. But assuming that the representation by

---

[5] This breakdown is suggested by Robert S. Weinberg, "The Uses and Limitations of Mathematical Models," in *Scientific Decision Making in Business,* ed. Abe Shuchman (New York: Holt, Rinehart & Winston, 1963).

modeling is understood, and its limitations are observed, the computer can carry out these operations easily and accurately. The importance of devoting careful extra effort to make sure that all factors are taken into account, in designing the model and specifying data needed, cannot be overemphasized.

OR FOR GROWTH—OR DISASTER

Operations research techniques can be applied to one project or small enterprises, and they can also be used in colossal undertakings, such as major conflicts between nations. It is there, perhaps, that the consequences of OR can be discerned most readily. This is particularly true when mistakes are made by planners and costly miscalculations result. The logistics planning for the Korean War, for instance, was based on World War II experience with several levels of supply points at corresponding echelons of command. The models used were backed up by the latest computer techniques then known and incorporated all possible communications and transportation facilities that would help keep them up to date. Unfortunately, the war differed in character from the one that was assumed in the model. The Korean terrain and geography differed from that of western Europe and the echelon concept proved faulty as the fighting front shifted. As a result, the elaborate logistics setup had to be scrapped and plans hastily revised. The basic differences in the types of wars being fought were again ignored in Vietnam, requiring other costly and hurried adjustments.

It would be incorrect to assume that systems analysis is useful only, or even primarily, in planning a war, studying the stock market, or streamlining a business operation. It can be used to tackle the broadest range of human problems. The Indus Plains Study in West Pakistan, for example, clearly illustrates how systems analysis can be used to combat human starvation and misery. Here the problem was to restore the productivity of one of the world's greatest river systems, the Indus River and its five tributaries, each in itself a major river, and each nourishing innumerable towns and cities. For more than a century, leaks had been appearing in the more than 10,000-mile network of canals that link the rivers and irrigate the Indus plains. The result had been an increasing elevation in the ground water table so that land that was once cultivated was becoming swampland and lakes. The increased water salinity that both damages plant roots and causes rapid evaporation was ruining about 100,000 acres a year.

A physical model representing the entire range of problems on the Indus plains could have been constructed. But it would have been far less flexible and adaptable than the computer model that was actually created, consisting of coded instructions on punched cards describing every sort of experimental approach. Without actually going to the expense and time of performing the experiments, the Indus plains computer study simulated the various ways the water table could be lowered—by drainage ditches, leak sealing in the canals, pumping out water by sinking wells, and so on. The plan eventually adopted proposed a grid of 32,000 wells covering about 25 million acres. The plan also recommended that each phase of the work should involve at least a million acres, to avoid water seepage from adjacent regions.

The full-scale engineering suggested by the computer has paid off. More than two million acres of land have thus far been recovered, an area capable of feeding four million additional people, and the water levels are falling at the predicted rate of 12 inches a year.

The Indus plains study involved a holistic approach, in which every possible contingency was allowed for. Of course, it requires continuing analysis to make every allowance for changing conditions —the effects of new methods of cultivation, fertilizers, insecticides, roads, pumping stations, human occupation, and the like.

In contrast to the Indus plains study, another project, the Aswan Dam in Egypt, shows how disastrous can be the failure to use the systems analysis approach in solving problems. The dam was built at a tremendous cost to provide more cultivable land and electricity for adjacent areas. What was not foreseen, but could have been predicted by systems analysis, was that the dam would alter the course of the tributary rivers of the Nile and change the chemical content of their water. Today, the salt content of this water has risen to dangerous levels, harmful to plants and thus worse than useless for irrigation. The quantity and variety of fish are diminishing. Simultaneously, bilharzia, the snail-borne disease, is on the increase because the traditional one-crop irrigation process has been replaced by four-crop rotation. Nutriments deposited annually by the Nile flood are severely depleted, and this is reducing the fertility of the soil. Already, the changes wrought by the dam have had unfortunate effects on the fisheries of the eastern Mediterranean.

The results of this project are likely to be ultimately catastrophic. Yet they could have been foreseen and prevented if long-range planning had been substituted for shortsighted, short-term vision. Had a systems analysis study been carried out long before the first spadeful of earth was moved, the story would have been very different. Quite probably no dam would have been built, and a massive program of population control would have been mounted in its stead. In some instances, making more land available for cultivation may be the worst thing for a nation to do. Where before there were only a small number of people living on the edge of starvation, unplanned soil recovery may cause a substantial increase in the number of people who more than ever continue to live near the edge of starvation.

There are numberless examples of undertakings being disastrously affected by someone's failure to consider all relevant factors. It is most often changes—in technology, in the environment, and so forth—that account for the problems and our failure to solve them.

Much of the human confusion so common in society today can be attributed to the inexorable rate at which change is occurring. Over the last 20 to 25 years, there has probably been more change than over all previous recorded human history—and it is technology, and to an increasing extent, computer technology, that has caused the changes. Yet, computer technology has also provided the physical basis needed for the effective use of systems analysis. Thus, it has provided us with hope for the future, as well as temporary current confusion. Future progress in forecasting and better planning of what is to come will help us avoid some of the human anxiety and confusion caused by a fast-changing technology. As Alvin Toffler has emphasized in *Future Shock,* "schools for the future" rank high among our needs for the means with which to cope with this swiftly changing world.

THE COMPUTER AND SOCIETY

The potential powers of the computer and of computerized problem-solving techniques are so enormous that there has been an increasing amount of discussion concerning the role of the computer in society. There have, for instance, been doubts expressed, largely because of fears of lost privacy, as to whether it was either wise or even legal for computers to be used in certain types of research. These doubts reflect the concern felt at society's highest levels, and much of this concern applies to the whole of technology, rather than to computer systems alone. It is reflected in the transcripts of hearings of various learned or official bodies. Among these is the Subcommittee on Science, Research, and Development of the Committee on Science and Astronautics of the House of Representatives. The subcommittee has published *Technology Assessment Seminar,* a report that contains prepared statements by several noted scholars and administrators.

Among those who contributed to the report was Dr. Emmanuel G. Mesthene, executive director, Program on Technology and Society, Harvard University, who pointed out the importance to our future of the "social role of knowledge." Another witness was Professor Melvin Kranzberg, Department of Humanities and Social Studies, Program in Science, Technology, and Public Policy, Case Institute of Technology of Case Western Reserve University. He stated:

> Instead of mere cost-benefit analysis, I should like to see technological developments steered toward desirable social and practical goals. And, when a technological advance clearly leads to intolerable consequences, I should like to hear someone in authority say "no" clearly and in advance. And when they lead to sound social consequences, I should like to hear somebody in authority say "yes." Constructive technology assessment is far better and more valuable than negative assessments.

Dr. Kranzberg also pointed out that computers can participate through model-building and simulation in what he calls second-order technology assessment. "Severe social dislocation might be identified. Corrective ideas could be tried. At the end the systems researchers might have some very practical ideas about the second-order effects . . . in advance of the final design and production." The subcommittee, at the time chaired by Congressman Emilio Q. Daddario, is pursuing its self-appointed task to ". . . integrate science and engineering into public policy on a more completely informed basis."

Elsewhere in the government, a long-range look at the broad questions of societal problem solving is being taken by the Office of Science and Technology, Executive Office of the President. Answers are being sought to such questions as finding new ways of ordering our national priorities, defining the role of technology, and determining how to apply the systems approach.

Also being carried out within the Office of Science and Technology is a methodology study of technology assessment. Its stated objectives are to "delineate where existing analytical or institutional processes can be applied or could be made to apply if modified, to ascertain where new processes must be developed, and actually to develop such new processes to the extent that time and funds permit." Within the framework of this effort, several pilot case studies are being developed, such as the one eloquently entitled, "Certain Aspects of the Impact of Computers on Society."

In a recent article, Gabor Strasser[6] has reported on several problems encountered by systems engineers studying urban or environmental issues. These are the decision-making, indicator, and long-range planning problems.

Of the three phases of the decision-making process—(1) deciding what should be done, (2) deciding how it should be done, and (3) taking necessary action to get it done—it is said that, too often, systems engineers can make their contribution only in the second phase. They are not participating sufficiently in "policy or objective formulation or with problems of implementation." The indicator problem—measures of output performance—has not been solved in either urban or environmental analysis because variables are hard to define or to measure. Long-range planning suffers from neglect because of pressure to "put out the fire," underfinancing, and the rate at which change is occurring in our complex world. Dr. Strasser offers suggestions and puts forward his belief that if the potential achievements in societal problem solving that the computer makes possible are to be realized, it is very much the business of universities, government agencies, and other organizations of all types to aid in this realization.

---

6 Gabor Strasser, "Impediments to Societal Problem Solving," *IEEE Spectrum* 8, no. 7 (July 1971).

10

Coping with the Computer

It took nearly a century for the first working version of the machine envisaged by Charles Babbage, the computer, to actually be completed. But, since 1946, computer developers have more than made up for the initial delay, and the computer and its characteristics have been improved at a staggering pace that still shows no sign of slackening.

The first widely used computer, the UNIVAC I, filled a very large room and cost over $1 million. By contrast, a modern computer with the same capacities would sell for only about $20,000 and would fit on a desktop. Since the UNIVAC I was first installed in 1951, the physical size of computers has gone down by a factor of about 1,000, with reliability increasing at the same rate, and costs dropping by a factor of 100. In 1955 the total U.S. population of installed computers had a rated capability of about one-half million additions per second. By 1965, it had increased to 200 million. At the rate at which the number of installed computers and their operating speeds keep increasing, this capacity will have grown about 400-fold.

Some perspective of the huge change that computers have brought to the economics of data handling is provided by a survey of the National Academy of Sciences. It states that the cost of making

125 million multiplications has steadily diminished from $12.5 million for a man working unaided, with pencil and paper, to $2.15 million for one using a desk calculator. The same work could be done by the first working computer, ENIAC, for a still hefty $130,000, but the cost then really dropped precipitously to the point where it could be done by the large-scale, second-generation IBM 7094 computer for only $132. A few years later, it was down to $4, using Control Data Corporation's giant third-generation machine, CDC 6600.

EQUIPMENT AND USAGE TRENDS

Computers will continue to become smaller, while their power increases. This is being accomplished through the steady reduction of the size of computer components, chiefly circuitry, and the development of new, more compact, ones. This trend was first known as "miniaturization," but, significantly, it is now called "microminiaturization." This change of label reflects the adoption in the late 1960s of a new concept in electronic circuitry, LSI (Large-Scale Integration). The LSI concept is now being perfected to the point where several hundred electronic circuit elements can now be packed on a minute (0.40 sq. in.) wafer, or chip, of silicone substrate. In the near future, this will be increased to several thousand. And, the only thing that stands in the way of ultimately turning jests about "computers on a chip" into reality is the need for electromechanical input and output devices and for manual controls.

By 1975 it is expected that computers will have decreased in size by a factor of about 100. This reduction will occur mainly in the size of computer memories. These are now relatively bulky arrays of ferrite cores arranged in high stacks. They will be gradually replaced by compact LSI semiconductor units. Smaller size will, however, be accompanied by bigger storage capacity that will rise to an average of 15 million characters. By comparison, the early first-generation computers could store only about 40,000 characters.

The internal operating speeds of computers are also expected to spurt ahead—rising by a factor of 200 between 1965 and 1975, permitting the performance of up to 4 million operations per second. In 1954 this rate was only about 2,000 operations per second, and it had risen only to 150,000 operations per second by 1964. As operating speeds continue to rise, per-instruction costs are going down.

In 1946 the cost of doing one million operations on the ENIAC keyboard topped $1,000 and the process took at least one month. In 1952 it was still nearly $300, although the time was now down to 10 minutes. Then in 1960 the price nosedived to $.75 and the job could be done in one second. Currently, the cost averages six cents and the time is about ½ of a second. Costs and speeds of one-tenth of a cent and one-tenth of a second are in sight. By 1997 the cost may have decreased by a factor of 100.

Improvements in computer capabilities and costs are being matched by developments in computer usage. For instance, the steady reduction of the cost of computers and related equipment is now making it cheaper to store information on magnetic tape and other memory devices rather than on paper. This means that the data bank concept is becoming economical and that computer storage can be used to hold more than just valuable or action data. Similarly, reduced costs are making it increasingly practical to use computer systems for new applications. Many of these are based on the use of communications that make the computer and its information available to many people in different locations.

Today nearly 25 percent of all computers handle some communications-based applications. By 1975 this proportion will have risen to 40 percent, and will cover more than half of all large computers. An early example is provided by the ARPA (Advanced Research Project Agency) network sponsored by the Department of Defense. The ARPA network links together universities and other research agencies to allow them to save money and speed efficiency by using the same computers, information, and software, independent of their location in the network.

In the future, networks similar to ARPA's will be organized on a commercial basis as information utilities, dispensing information and computing services, much as the electricity utilities deliver power. The means they will use to deliver information to their customers' homes or offices will be telephone lines, or microwave links, or, perhaps, some new delivery medium, such as cable television (CATV). In addition, a system of communications satellites may someday be in permanent orbit over the United States, providing vastly improved data processing, as well as telephone and television, service to the entire nation. The Federal Communications Commission has recommended that private companies be allowed to go into the communications satellite business. FCC officials foresee that, in time, there may be as many as four independent systems, each with its own satellite. Much of the traffic they will handle will come from overseas, because computers and computer communications are forging an increasingly tight worldwide web of information. Even the planning of new computers must now be done on an international basis—as in the case of IBM, whose final equipment designs must reflect information from at least 20 countries around the world, so that all their needs may be met. The new machines must be equally able to handle a variety of numbering systems, for instance, sterling as well as decimal figures, and their printers must come with type-faces for 22 different languages, ranging from English to Hebrew, Indian, or Japanese.

Computer communications represent a major trend for the future, and the question may be asked as to what will happen when terminals and data communications cross over from the gadgetry stage to becoming facts of everyday life. A lighthearted possible answer was provided in 1970 by *Dataweek*, the British computer publication.

By the year 2000, the working week had come down to 15 hours, except for computer people. Theirs ranged from 10 to 80 according to the employer and the basis of remuneration.

Internationally, the U.S. Census Bureau created a system with up-to-date records for all the 400 million citizens, including their bank balances, their tax returns for 20 years, their mistresses and lovers, and the number of fillings in their teeth.

Britain opted for a more discreet approach that omitted the mistresses and lovers. The French assumed the existence of M's and L's and incorporated a random number generator that allowed citizens the tax and bank returns they wanted on file.

The Russians produced a system with a political code that permitted names to be inadvertently lost in the system without disturbing associated data. The Chinese simply went on producing more Chinese.

Between testimony sessions for the nine committees appointed to investigate intrusion of privacy, man looked at his terminal and found it good. . . .

CAN WE DO WITHOUT THE COMPUTER?

In the 1950s, when computers were first being introduced on a significant scale, their promoters used to cite impressive calculations, forecasts of what would happen if computers had not been developed. Among them was the "paper tiger" forecast in which it was argued that the nation's paperwork was growing at such a rate that without computers, by the late 1950s, every man, woman, and child in the United States would be busy all day coping with this paperwork. The forecast, of course, did not stand up. If there had been no computers, then we would simply not have done (or probably generated) the extra paperwork. Our lives might be poorer, but we would have survived. Even so, it is estimated that in the U.S. the small businessman alone is required by his government to fill out some 15 million forms annually.

The increasing volume of paperwork is, however, only a symptom of a long-term trend that has governed the development of our society. This is a trend toward complexity, accompanied by increasing interdependence and by a spiraling growth of the number of individuals and organizations whose decisions have some bearing on the course of our affairs and of society as a whole. This has meant that the need for information and for its retrieval and processing has grown with this complexity, which is itself caused by the expansion of the supply of information.

Society's storehouse of knowledge has grown steadily larger throughout history. However, its dimensions and the demands made on it only became really significant in the past century with the establishment of compulsory education and the spread of general literacy throughout most of the Western World. Very soon, education, telephones, telegraphs, and all the other manifestations of information and communication, were seen as more than just luxuries. The demand for more and better information became steadily greater as decisions of all types—personal, business, political—became increasingly dependent on an expanding information flow.

There were two factors that caused the rising demand for reliable information. First, better, more plentiful information allowed decisions to be reached more surely and more readily. This, in turn, hastened the pace of change, rendering obsolete existing knowledge, and even our individual reactions to various situations. Secondly, with change, came increasing diversity of knowledge, work, life styles. The need for a greater flow of information also grew as the separate groups, while they became more diverse, also became more dependent on each other and thus had to engage in a constant exchange of information.

The spread of literacy, the use of computers, and the establishment of huge data banks and stores of information—all these do not mean that society now has too much information. Quite the opposite is true. There is far too little, for as new information becomes known, it itself generates new questions, new demands for yet more data. The scope and complexity of this information are more than matched by those of the society that demands it. There would be little chance of filling this demand without computers. We could do without them only if we accepted the full renunciation that this would imply— that of our way of life and our society as we know and apparently cherish them.

With computers, we can do things that we could never have done, unaided, otherwise. However, our growing dependence on the machines is not an unmixed blessing. The computer is such a powerful tool that we can fear its misuse no matter how inadvertent. For example, it is already becoming a basic tool of political campaigns, proving more effective than radio or television, but also creating the danger that no candidate can win who does not have access to computer support—yet another limitation on the equal opportunity to run for public office that is theoretically enjoyed by everyone in a democracy. In our dependence on the computer, we have passed the point of no return, but we are not always certain where we are heading.

THERE IS NO UTOPIA

Every new technology that man has created has at one time or another been hailed as the panacea that would at one stroke solve some of humanity's most pressing problems—preserving man from nature's caprices and from his own folly alike. The printing press, the factory system, the rise of literacy, the telephone, radio, and television—they all in their time have been hailed as instruments of prosperity through whose use we would soon reach a nearby utopia.

Even the lighter-than-air balloon was in its day regarded as an instrument for universal peace because, it was believed that nations, being able to observe one another, would lose the advantage of surprise. The use of aerial projectiles was discounted because it would make war "too horrible."[1] The balloon never lived up to its early billing, but whenever a technology has gained wide acceptance, it has generally been found that its use created new problems that were sometimes even more serious than those it was designed to solve. The invention of printing in China, for instance, was accompanied by the production of enormous quantities of worthless paper currency by Kublai Khan's successors, creating history's first paper money inflation, and causing the ouster of China's Mongol overlords. In the West, the pious churchmen who were among the first customers for the religious works turned out on crude hand presses could not know that soon a flood of printed heretical literature and polemics of all sorts would hasten the disunity of Christendom, effectively signifying the end of the traditional medieval society.

Computer technology has, like its predecessors, been oversold. Like them, it has created new problems at the same time that it helped solve old ones. Even the solving of those old problems has not always been entirely beneficial. In the area of privacy, for instance, the individual citizen's chief protection has historically been the inefficiency with which data was formerly collected, handled, and classified. Now that detailed sensitive information is on file for nearly everyone, access to that data must be carefully guarded, but this is proving very difficult. In fact, would-be privacy invaders often find it far easier to rifle computer data banks than do the latter's guardians in restricting access. Even the most ingenious technical safeguards are found to have drawbacks. Voice recognition, for instance, would seem to hold promise, with access to its stored information being granted by the computer only to those whose voice tones it can recognize as those of authorized personnel. However, most of the original research used only male voices and the technique works poorly with female voices unless a system is designed exclusively for them. Bad colds and hay fever represent other prob-

---

1 The only significant use of balloons for aerial bombardment, during the mid-19th century siege of Venice by the Austrians, had relatively little impact. However, at the turn of the century, H. G. Wells, the British writer, could still predict, in his book *War in the Air*, the destruction of human civilization as a result of worldwide conflicts between fleets of lighter-than-air warcraft.

lems, and a major corporation could thus run the risk of finding itself out of business when the pollen count went up.

It is perhaps no wonder that a good many of the more than 1,000 unsolicited suggestions that IBM receives every year describe the same data terminal personal identification scheme. Under it, anyone wishing to use the terminal must first enter his or her thumb into a small box containing an identification device, and if it is the wrong thumb, a guillotine blade comes down to create a disposal problem.

The example of the thumb and the guillotine blade outlines with grim humor the great and urgent problem that accompanies computer usage, that of *interface*. Just as surely as the guillotine blade will chop off an unauthorized intruding thumb, so the computer will prove to be a source of bewilderment, and even of sorrow, whenever it is misused, whether with malice or with ineptitude. The need for a solution to this problem is a pressing one. Paradoxically, this urgency comes from the continuing extension of the systems approach, and the organization of our society increasingly takes the form of man-machine systems. This partnership of human beings and computers could promise infinite betterment for mankind if man's understanding of how to use the computer was a well-balanced one. However, it is not, and the consequences of poorly designed or misused systems can be far worse than those of unsupported human action. In commercial terms, if a product is lost, a company can be lost, but on a higher level, if a system is lost, then an entire nation can be lost.

The interface problem is basically a human one, and its solution can best be found through appropriate action in three basic areas of human activities: education, legislation, and professional leadership.

EDUCATION—MEN MUST KNOW

There is no general agreement as to what will be the ultimate role of the computer on our society, but it is clear that it will be a fundamental one. Simon Ramo, in his book, *Century of Mismatch*, has outlined how great may be the consequences and how much they may differ: "By the turn of the century, all we may have is a clear trend toward a robot society, or toward a society that uses technology to gain a higher degree of freedom for the individual. But such a trend may be set quite strongly, even irrevocably, in the near future, and there is no point in risking it. We ought to understand the alternatives now, and we ought to work to achieve the one we want."

Obviously, the way to understand the alternatives so that we may achieve the best kind of society is through education and indoctrination, starting with society's current leaders—at the very highest levels of business, government, and industry. If they are to make the right decisions, these men and women must know the fundamentals of the new computerized techniques that can make the planning and management functions more creative and efficient. They should at least be aware of how they can benefit from the understanding and use of these techniques. For instance, to make the right decisions, individuals must have up-to-date and reliable information, and they must be able to evaluate properly the frequently complex alternatives that this information may impose. There is increasingly little possibility that our society's leaders can make their decisions quickly and accurately without adopting a systems outlook to simplify complexity. The need for their doing so is all the more pressing in that their decisions must ever more frequently be those of how to protect society from the possible effects of planned or existing systems. To achieve the proper understanding, they must be made aware of the ways in which different professional disciplines interact and of the high levels of synthesis and forecasting that can be reached through application of the systems and analytic sciences. Then, they must balance this awareness with information about just what the computer can do and cannot do—its maximum scope and its very real limitations.

The job of indoctrinating society's leaders about the computer should be that of the computer professionals. Several organizations have initiated programs, some quite ambitious, to make the public at all levels aware of the nature and potential of the computer and computer-related techniques. Among them is the Harvard University Program on Technology and Society, which under the leadership of Dr. Emmanuel G. Mesthene, has carried out an investigation of the impact on society of technological change. In his book, *Technological Change: Its Impact on Man and Society*,[2] Dr. Mesthene presented his view of the nature of technological change, describing it as made up of three chief aspects: social changes, values, and

2 (New York: New American Library, 1970).

economic and political organization. Each of these aspects represents only a part of the entire phenomenon, and they, themselves, can be broken down further into even more limited "one-dimensional" views. For instance, he points out that there are at least three narrow views that can be held concerning technological change, each containing its share of truth and distortions to see it as a blessing, a curse, or of no particular importance. Thus, he says, "Technological change creates new opportunities and new problems at the same time and in virtue of each other."

Dr. Mesthene's work is intended to guard us against taking a lopsided "one-dimensional" view of change, and lead us instead to appreciate the interdisciplinary nature of systematic inquiry for the solution of any problem. Thus, complex changes that affect large numbers of people and embrace many unrelated activities of society must be jointly examined by teams of scientists, economists, and political leaders—using analytic techniques to permit them to assess the broad implications of these changes for society. Decision makers must know how to handle these techniques if they are to retain the full breadth of their vision.

Work is now being done by the government to provide federal managers with greater knowledge of computers so that they may use them to maximum advantage. In 1965 the U.S. Civil Service Commission established an ADP Management Training Center in Washington, D.C. Outside the government, the bulk of the effort must be shouldered by the computer professionals. Panels of speakers must be created to provide unbiased information on all phases of the technology. The mystery and misunderstanding surrounding the computer must be dispelled, and the fundamental principles of automation must be made easy to understand. Each industry should be analyzed dynamically, and its leaders should be acquainted with the role of automation and information processing in their industry. Politicians, union leaders, and industrial managers, who often have most to say about economic decisions affecting us all, must be given the basis for making sensible estimates of the future impact of automation.

Much has been done already by the professional associations. The American Federation of Information Processing Societies and its member organizations have created speaker bureaus. However, more deliberate, organized effort is called for. More specific industry breakdowns, with greater specialization and local effort, can bring more personal, individualized messages closer to home. Government agencies such as the Department of Health, Education, and Welfare, Office of Education, and the Departments of Commerce and Labor, can help by coordinating contacts within government and with industry and labor. Investigating panels and subcommittees of congressional committees have shown increasing awareness of the ramifications of science and technology, with a heavy emphasis on automation, computers, and information systems. This concern is evidence of a growing awareness of the importance of long-range planning and the use of the systems approach in preparing for the impact of technological change. However, only a small beginning has been made as yet. Much work remains to be done in indoctrinating the leaders in most areas of business, government, and industry.

Indoctrination and training efforts must be made at all levels of society, particularly in the case of those workers who are displaced by automation. Their number is limited. The threat of technological unemployment has failed to take on the dimensions that had been predicted in the early 1950s. However, a small number of workers have inevitably lost their employment thereby, and even a few are too many—and the impact of their displacement is far greater than their number would explain.

Paradoxically, one of the most promising areas of employment for men and women who have been displaced by automation is automation itself. Thus, if these men and women are found to have the proper aptitudes, they may find jobs that require less manual dexterity, but greater mental skills, as in the case of a highly automated plant where even the simpler operations will require the operator to understand fully its functions and controls. A vigorous testing program is very important. For instance, persons with superior aptitudes for symbol manipulation can aspire to jobs as computer operators or programmers, with suitable training. And, for the latter, local adult training programs must also be initiated on a more ambitious scale. However, if this is done, it must be remembered that the only foolproof motivation for the trainees is their sure knowledge that there are actually jobs to be had at the completion of their training.

Many colleges and universities now offer computer courses. There is, however, still more they could do to prepare students for a world deep in the throes of change, much of which is being caused by automation. Courses should be offered that stress applications, information systems, computer engineering logic, and the fundamentals of computer economics. The college undergraduate should soon acquire a sense of proportion concerning computers—for example, what they can and cannot do, and why[2]; how they can be misused; and probable near-future developments, uses, and consequences in computer technology. To satisfy these needs, students should be given more courses than those now available, on the fundamentals of computer logic and programming and other basic but narrow technical aspects of the subject. They should also be trained in systems analysis, which is quite as important a subject as the fundamentals of logic and numerical representation. As balanced and well-thought-out courses of this type are developed, our educational institutions will turn out new crops of leaders of industry and government who will feel no need for the indoctrination that our present leaders lack.

At the high school level, computer programming courses for beginners have been offered, often spurred on by pioneering work in this area by local chapters of the Association for Computing Machinery and supported by a vigorous program of the national organization. Some brilliant work has been done by high school students. This educational preparation could be rounded out through greater emphasis, at both the high school and elementary school levels, on discussions of the role of computers and automation, and explanations of how computers work and of the nature and use of binary notation. This can be strengthened by field trips, by demonstrations, and, where suitable, by "hands-on" experience.

One of the most glaring indications of the failure of our educational system is provided by the great amount of "unlearning" that one must undertake when encountering the binary environment of computer technology without adequate prior preparation. This is another manifestation of the interface problem, a highly visible one, but one that we should find reasonably easy to eliminate.

LEGISLATION—SAFEGUARDS FOR INDIVIDUALS

Laws are traditionally difficult to change, and the need for new laws must sometimes be painfully apparent before action is taken. Due

[2] See I. J. and M. Wilson, *What Computers Cannot Do* (Princeton: Auerbach Publishers, 1970); and M. J. Cooper, *What Computers Can Do* (Princeton: Auerbach Publishers, 1969).

deliberation and proper care are important in the formulation of new legislation. This deliberation has been much in evidence in the formulation of new laws with which to deal with new computer-related situations. This deliberation has been thoroughly justified because the technological and usage picture has been changing at a rate far faster than that with which the legislative process has been able to keep up. An example of this is the still-pending new copyright legislation, which has been repeatedly subjected to committee hearings in Congress during the past six or seven years. The clash of conflicting interests among educators, broadcasters, and publishers has contributed to this delay. But the changing technologies of the print-copying, computing, and communications industries, which provided much of the impetus for a new copyright law, have also been responsible for some of the changes and additions being made in committee even now. The House of Representatives Committee on the Judiciary indicated this in its Report No. 83, *Copyright Law Revision*, March 8, 1967, p. 24: "Recognizing the profound impact that information storage and retrieval devices seem destined to have on authorship, communications, and human life itself, the committee is also aware of the dangers of legislating prematurely in this area of exploding technology."

Sometimes, however, legislators have been inclined to apply this kind of deliberation in the face of urgent needs, and to prevent or delay consideration of needed legislative proposals. New legislation is needed to deal with the extensive damage now made possible by the new electronic technologies. The computer provides us with great benefits and makes our lives easier and more efficient through its capabilities for collection, processing, editing, storage, and retrieval of vast volumes of information. However, the possibilities of harm to individuals and organizations being caused through the accidental or deliberate misuse of this stored data must be dealt with and more positive and effective action must be taken than has been done to date. So far, loud denunciations of possible breaches of privacy have headed off projects such as the National Data Center. These, however, have been largely negative achievements. Positive action needs to be taken in the form of legislation that will go further than the well-meaning reforms, largely in the area of credit reporting, that have yet been enacted.

Among the most vigilant congressional watchdogs on the subject of privacy is Senator Sam Ervin, who, for several years, has been the chairman of the Subcommittee on Constitutional Rights, in the section of Effects on Individuals. According to Senator Ervin's statement to the Senate on 8 February 1971, the subcommittee goal is:

> To learn, first, what government data banks have been developed; second, how far they are already computerized or automated; third, what constitutional rights, if any, are affected by them; and fourth, what overall legislative controls, if any, are required.

From this statement of the subcommittee's goal, and in keeping with the normal interests of legislators, a law resulting from these hearings and studies is likely to stress broad principles and responsibilities for insuring protection of citizens' rights, rather than technical details of specific methods and mechanisms to carry out the responsibilities. Presumably, therefore, this law would assign responsibility for administration of its provisions, or create a new agency for the purpose.

Professor Arthur Miller, of the University of Michigan Law School and author of *The Assault on Privacy*, in his testimony at hearings held by Senator Ervin's subcommittee, advocated creation of a separate government agency to direct the proposed new Federal Data Center. Other witnesses called to provide information concerning the technical problems included an official of the IBM Corporation; Robert Henderson, vice-president of the Honeywell Corporation; Robert Bigelow, chairman of the Committee on Computers and Society of the Association for Computing Machinery; and Caxton C. Foster, a professor of computer science.

Many other studies and investigations have been conducted on data gathering and centralized or coordinated management and use of economic and personal data. In the late 1960s, Robert L. Chartrand, Information Sciences Specialist in the Science Policy Research Division of the Library of Congress, prepared a summary of such studies relating to the then proposed Federal Data Center. The report, entitled *The Federal Data Center: Proposals and Reactions* (TK 6565C, SP 137, 14 June 1968), commented on the following investigations that have provided basic material for much of the work now being done on the subject:

1. Committee on the Preservation and Use of Economic Data (Chairman: Richard Ruggles). Report to the Social Sciences Research Council. Washington, D.C., April 1965.

2. Edgar S. Dunn, Jr. Review of proposal for a national data center. Bureau of the Budget. December 1965.

3. Cornelius E. Gallagher. Questions of invasion of privacy relating to the establishment of a national data center. (Remarks in the House, 21 October, 1966.) Also: other remarks, letter, news release, 1966, 1967.

4. Task Force on the Storage of and Access to Government Statistics (Chairman: Carl Kaysen, Chairman of the Institute for Advanced Study at Princeton). Report of the Task Force to the Bureau of the Budget. Washington, October 1966.

5. Congress. House. Committee on Government Operations. Special Subcommittee on Invasion of Privacy. (Chairman: Senator Edward V. Long) The computer and invasion of privacy. Hearings, July 26-28, 1966.

In his summary of the several investigations dealing with the pros and cons of the projected Federal Data Center, Mr. Chartrand also refers to the so-called Freedom of Information Act, passed in 1966. This act "provides that information and records be made available to the general public except for certain categories of data." Invasion of personal privacy is prevented by requesting agencies to delete identifying details; categories exempted include personal and medical files and investigation files compiled for law enforcement. But the act does not define considerations involved in handling computerized information.

It is apparent that new legislation is needed. However, it is perhaps not so apparent that more technical spadework must be done before such legislation can be formulated and an agency set up to administer its provisions. Foolproof methods of insuring the privacy and security of information systems must be developed and proven. What is needed, rather than scattered achievements, is the development of uniform standards of effectiveness and of a commonly accepted scale with which to rank different security schemes if effective legislation is to be drafted. In addition to the usual authentication and memory-protection techniques, it should be possible to provide in multiuser systems a sort of technical "police protection" by built-in alarms that alert authorities when serious violations are detected. It will surely be necessary for responsible technical experts, representing the several segments of the information-processing community—hardware manufacturers, software developers, service system operators, system users—to form a commission composed of a number of working panels, to attack these and other technical problems.

Draft legislation that will provide adequate safeguards against the misuse of computers in diminishing the humanity, the independence, and the integrity of man should include the following provisions:

1. No organization shall be permitted to maintain personal data files on more than half a million individuals. All data collection organizations shall be subject to the strictest licensing and periodic inspection.

2. All information shall be held strictly confidential, with safeguards against unauthorized and improper circulations. It shall be considered a criminal offense, punishable by fine and imprisonment, to make unauthorized use of such information.

3. Information given to any data collection organization, governmental or otherwise, shall not be used or circulated for any purpose unless the identity of the individuals or group supplying the information is completely removed from the supplied information, or they consent to such use.

4. It shall be unlawful for any agency to ask or require answers to questions relating to race, ethnicity, religion, free speech, and other personal matters.

5. It shall be the right of every citizen to know who supplied any kind of information about himself or his family, and to have the right to question or rebut such information.

6. It shall be the right of every citizen to have access to his own file, to question and correct questionable and inaccurate entries, and to place certain restrictions on access by others to his file.

7. Whenever an individual's file is consulted, the name of the consulting individual and of the person authorizing his access shall be permanently recorded.

8. Illicit access to a file, or the obtaining of personal information by deceit, shall be considered a crime and a civil wrong, punishable by fine and/or imprisonment. The offender shall be suable by the injured party for invasion of privacy and have damages awarded against him.

9. The files shall be exempt from a court's subpoena.

10. There shall be a committee or ombudsman to hear criticisms and complaints on the use of files, to rectify any wrongs or errors, and to receive and send to the appropriate authority the necessary recommendations for improving the system.

To guard against illicit tapping of computer information, all computers should be designed with safeguards against such activities. Various cryptographic protections might be used to modify the signals so that they could not be readily deciphered by the tapper. Other efficient protective devices must also be designed. It has also been suggested that "passkeys," which would enable only properly authorized persons to use computer storage, would help safeguard information. There are many possibilities; their development is simply a matter of time. Such safeguards must be maintained and improved in order to permit the calm and steady expansion of the beneficial uses of the computer.

PROFESSIONAL LEADERSHIP

Computing technology today holds an enormous potential for improvement of man and his way of life. The development of this potential, however, is hobbled by widespread ignorance concerning computers and their use, and the frequent instances of and opportunities for misuse of the computer. It is clear that leaders must be found to show the way out of this dilemma, and no one is better able to provide such leadership than the computer professionals.

The leadership role that computer professionals must play is not a novel one in any other profession. In all of them, it is normal for individuals who are interested in furthering the progress of their various specialties to participate in such supporting activities as training, indoctrination, the organization of formal courses, public speaking, and writing—all intended to strengthen communications inside their profession and to establish bridges of understanding between the profession and the general public.

Most important, perhaps, engineers, mathematicians, and other computer professionals must provide formal support for the development of the necessary standards and other tools of the profession—so that society may feel confidence in the reliability of these tools. Older professional organizations developed standards for such things as thread sizes in mechanical tools, and, for the electrical industry, Underwriters Laboratories provided definitions, standards, and inspection procedures. The computer industry is being faced with similar requirements.

Every industry, and each specialty within a major industry, develops its own language, units of materials and workload, management-reporting customs, and communications codes. Thus chemical firms have systems for representing and transmitting chemical formulas and equations. For computer processing purposes, they have devised specialized procedures and codes, which would not be useful in other fields. In legal work, specialized notation for case citations, statute references, and constitutional interpretations exist, which facilitate the use of computer processing. Similarly, the peculiar language requirements of other industries compel the particular development of specialized codes and computer-oriented procedures. To avoid wasteful duplication, such efforts are frequently coordinated or consolidated within each major technological specialty.

Present standards activity in the computing and information sciences is sponsored and controlled by the American National Standards Institute (formerly USA Standards Institute), whose members include industrial firms, trade associations, technical societies, consumer organizations, and government agencies. Part-time activities of committee and subcommittee members constitute the major source of standards contributions. Progress is therefore limited to what can be accomplished at committee meetings, supplemented by the voluntary time of employees of member associations. A professionally staffed, full-time activity would therefore be justified, to speed the creation and implementation of standards of codes and procedures in each field. The following activities might be undertaken by full-time professionals for each industry specialty:

- —classification of each field into subfields
- —definitions of materials and processes
- —assignment of codes for efficient machine representation
- —creation and formalization of standards for weights, measures, and packaging
- —identification, definition, and structuring of specific information useful in management reporting systems
- —refinement of indexing and cross-reference terms for information retrieval
- —maintenance and cross-reference of files of standard computer program files

Certain types of studies must be conducted for the computing profession as a whole, but the individuals best suited to do them might be some of those involved in the industry specialties, that is, subject-matter specialists rather than computer specialists. For such purposes, selected persons should be assigned to serve as members of interdisciplinary teams. There is, for instance, the difficult problem of identifying and subdividing areas of responsibility for computer malfunctions, for legal purposes. If damages must be adjudicated and assessed because of the malfunctioning of a computer system, the specific level of system malfunction, if known, may pinpoint the responsible person, equipment, or process. Since this is directly and intimately related to hardware and software functioning in specific programs, experts close to or capable of understanding their inter-relations must be involved.

The need for computer professionals to assume leading roles in computer education has already been stressed. Pioneering work at several levels has already been done by members of the Association for Computing Machinery, and other organizations, including curriculum revisions and volunteer lecturing, particularly at the high school level. However, the more difficult job of indoctrinating management-level and policy-making people requires additional attention. The American Management Association has been doing such work for some five years. Computing and engineering professionals should take a more active part in this as an organized effort jointly with representatives of AMA and other management associations. Policy makers in fields not ordinarily connected with business management must be reached. These include those in municipal and state governments, education, research, and philanthropic institutions, and politicians at all levels. Education must build a bridge connecting the old ways of making decisions and the new world of computers and the systems approach. Also, while not really classified as "education," consultation with legislators and testifying before congressional committees, by responsible computer and engineering professionals, help in accomplishing similar purposes.

Fundamental studies are needed, to round out or complement researches normally undertaken by commercial computer manufacturers and by the federal government. For example, we have been hearing about the lack of a satisfactory theory of computation.

In addition to fulfilling the researcher's need for theoretical under-pinning, work in this area could provide the practical limits of special-ization of instruction sets, better understanding of microprogram-ming, and a tie-in with information theory and communications principles. Another area for study is the potentially powerful field of hybrid machines, such as general-purpose computers created to serve specialized markets. This approach is all the more rewarding because the machines' special-purpose features are ever more specifi-cally tailored to particular applications or industries. The increasing trends toward miniaturization and other engineering developments point to the practicality of many new developments of this type in the near future.

There are many areas where computer technology has potential for harm to society—employment dislocation, dehumanization in some business relationships, invasions of privacy, unethical appli-cations. The professionals in computation, engineering. and infor-mation systems have a responsibility for pursuing solutions to such problems and for assisting the general public in understanding and accepting recommended solutions when they are developed. The other responsibilities, such as educating, assisting in drafting new legislation, and development of industry standards in codes, methods for measurement, and program evaluation, also require specific dele-gation of organized effort and methods for coordination.

In an industry whose annual gross is expressed in billions of dollars, there is an urgent need for creation of an Institute for Com-puter Research and Development. Such an institution should be sup-ported by private industry as a means of regulating its own orderly development and to render unnecessary the creation of too-strict, or too-little-and-too-late governmental regulation. Contributions from hardware and software firms in proportion to gross income, plus similar support from other industries interested in standardization and other computer-related services, should carry the financial bur-den. The organization, the professional staffing, and overall direction could be undertaken by a board created jointly by members of the American Federation of Information Processing Societies.

The principal purposes of the institute would be to undertake theoretical researches of the kind briefly mentioned previously, to develop drafts of standards for notation and mensuration within industry specialties, and to develop and promulgate technical and legal safeguards for society in relation to computer and systems operations. Additional functions could be considered, in the areas of guiding support for educational and indoctrinational requirements, development of standards for licensing and certifying computer professionals, and assisting in the drafting of legislation. A guiding overall principle should be to serve as an alert watchdog over developing potential troubles, for the purpose of smoothing out the rough spots, particularly at points of contact (interfaces) with society in general.

11

The Computer and the
Nature of Man

The computer is often cited as an example to support the thesis that a new technology will be exploited to its fullest possible extent as soon as it is developed. We are reminded that electronics was still largely a forced-growth development of World War II when ENIAC first went on the air, while among the transistors' most important initial applications were their use in second-generation computers. Yet, there are others who discount this thesis. The emphasis of technological development, they claim, may be chiefly governed by man's immediate needs and, even more, by his basic nature, rather than by mere feasibility. Thus, they say, while development is surging ahead in electronics in general, and computing in particular, no such impetus is apparent for some of the "soft" or social sciences, where major achievements have long been feasible. City planning, for instance, is one of the oldest sciences (or arts) known to man. The ancient Egyptians, Greeks, and Romans, among others, not to mention the men of the Renaissance and the Enlightenment, all wrote extensively on the subject and even occasionally practiced it. Yet, in our urban squalor, where are we now?

If the development of the computer is receiving such a high priority, it must be because through the computer, man gains unique powers that he has always sought with which to control his environment. This places the computer in a very special relationship to man, one that reflects his nature and, also, his origins, the way that he came up in the world—for man is the world's greatest social (or is it zoological?) climber. The nature of this climb, the challenge that started it, and the form of man's response all made it almost inevitable that the computer would be developed at some time in man's history.

A VERY DIFFERENT PRIMATE

The conditions that formed man and that led ultimately to the development of the computer began between two to five million years ago. Zoologists and anthropologists were understandably absent then, but if one had been present about that time, he might well have noted with interest the unusual behavior of what until then had been a rather unremarkable member of the fauna of the period. The end result could well have been a scholarly dissertation, entitled "Man, a Very Different Primate."

Man is but one of about 150 different species of living primates. However, he differs from them in two basic respects. He is one of the very few who is not a forest dweller, and he is the only one who is not predominantly vegetarian.

The reason why the other primates have an almost exclusively vegetarian diet is easy to understand. Plant food is so abundant in forests that it is more than sufficient to sustain life, supplemented occasionally with insects, small birds, lizards, eggs, and so on. This situation, where survival is basically assured, is idyllic, calling for little effort to develop or grow on the part of the forest creatures. The descriptions we have of the Garden of Eden are not too dissimilar. But, just as man was expelled from the Garden of Eden, according to the Bible, so was he stripped of his forest environment as climatic changes gradually deforested large areas of land in Africa south of the equator.

The savanna on which man now lived was semiarid, and its vegetation could not support even a small population. The man-like apes that lived in this gradually changing habitat were thus forced to modify their food-gathering habits to include animals. Thus, they added to their traditional diets of plants small, slow-moving animals or very young ones, and then the size of their prey began to increase as they actively took up hunting.

The consequences of man's turning to hunting were more than just dietary. The requirements of a hunting life placed a high premium on the ability to solve problems and to store all necessary information concerning the conduct of the hunt and, also, other human affairs as they became increasingly formalized in nature and, hence, data-rich. In effect, man's brain was starting to undertake the basic functions that, today, computer systems perform for man to supplement his brain.

As man developed, such instincts as may have remained to him gradually disappeared because they could no longer be of any use in an environment in which adaptation requires thinking and the successful meeting of a multiplicity of varying challenges. As instincts are dropped, everything that one learns is now learned from other human beings. The contributions that the individual makes to the stock of traditional knowledge also have to be learned by others. Therefore, the human brain must grow ever larger to serve as an information processing and retrieval center, a feature that characterizes the human species. It also ensured that, ultimately, man's information requirements would be such that the unaided human brain could no longer satisfy them. Then, the first crude artificial aids, be they pebbles, scratches on a bone, or scratches in the earth, would in time be succeeded by the computer.

THE LEARNING PROCESS

Learning begins at birth as information is imparted to a still immature brain. This brain has grown rapidly at the fetal stage, jumping from about 90 grams to from 350 to 400 grams in the last three months of intrauterine life (see table 11-1). At the rate that its brain is growing, the baby has to be born at the end of about 270 days; otherwise its head would be too large to pass through the birth canal. However, at the time of birth, the baby is still not really mature, and it takes another 270 days, on the average, to complete its gestation outside the womb to the point where the baby can crawl unaided. The brain also continues to grow and has virtually attained its adult size by the time the child is three years old. This growth reflects the fundamental learning that the child must achieve during

the first three years of his or her life. This is a fact that is too seldom
understood or appreciated. Learning naturally takes place throughout human existence, but the first half-dozen years of the child's life
are fundamental for the most important part of his learning process—
learning how to be human.

TABLE 11-1.   GROWTH OF THE HUMAN BRAIN

FETUS	WEIGHT (GRAMS)	GAIN (GRAMS)	
5 mos.	62.5	25.5	
6 mos.	88.0	25.5	
8 mos.	277.0	189.0	In this 2-month period, a tripling in weight and doubling increment
birth	350/392	73/115	An increment of about one-third its previous month's weight
6 mos.	656.0	306.0	Almost doubles in weight in first 6 months
12 mos.	825.0	169.0	In this period, reduced to one-half rate of increase in first 6 months
2 yrs.	1010.00	185.0	In this period, reduced to one-half rate of increase in first 6 months
3 yrs.	1115.00	105.0	In this period, reduced to one-third rate of increase in first 6 months
4 yrs.	1180.00	75.0	
6 yrs.	1250.00	70.0	
9 yrs.	1307.00	57.0	
12 yrs.	1338.00	31.0	
20-29 yrs.	1390.00	58.0	

Because he has so much to learn, the child is utterly dependent,
principally on his mother, for continued existence over long periods.
These periods include infancy, childhood, and adolescence, develop-
mental periods that are far more extended for man than for any
other species. Just as a computer constitutes a system for the handling
of information, the dependency of the child also builds up into a system of feedback relationship. As a result, the more extended is the
child's dependency, the greater are the evolutionary pressures that
emphasize in women the traits that best help fill their dependent
children's needs. The fetus's symbiotic relationship with its mother
is thus continued into the postnatal stage.

The relationship that exists between mother and child provides a good example of how inferior are, for all their power, the abilities of the computer to those of man. The electronic computer requires programs and instructions to be prepared by human beings and entered into it before it can operate. On the other hand, the general-purpose, biological computer that is man, or woman, is entirely self-programming in its development of the most effective means with which to ensure the healthy development and the survival of the human species. These means, taken together, are called—the ability to love.

Love represents the most powerful of humanity's information media, packing so much data into one brief response as to make the computer's binary notation seem rambling and gothically discursive. The mother teaches her infant how to love by expressing her own love through tactile, gustatory, visual, auditory, and other responses to his needs. The infant thereby gains the sensitivity, and the need for integration of these repeated experiences of love into his own system of loving responses. In short, the child learns how to love through direct experience. It is love that humanizes the child, the child that is father to the man.

THE INFORMATION MEDIUM OF LOVE

No one has better described or defined the meaning of love than George Chapman (1559?-1634), the Elizabethan poet and playwright, friend and fellow actor of William Shakespeare. In his play *All Fools*, first staged in 1595, Chapman has his hero say:

> I tell thee, Love is Nature's second Sun,
> Causing a spring of virtues where he shines;
> And as without the Sun, the World's great eye,
> All colours, beauties, both of art and Nature,
> Are given in vain to men; so without love
> All beauties bred in women are vain,
> All virtues born in men lie buried;
> For Love informs them as the Sun doth colours;
> And as the Sun, reflecting his warm beams
> Against the earth, begets all fruits and flowers;
> So love, fair shining in the inward man,
> Brings forth in him the honourable fruits
> Of valour, wit, virtue, and haughty thoughts,
> Brave resolution, and divine discourse.

A man, indeed, is the substance of the things he loves, and his identity as a person consists of the meaningfulness of his interrelationships. In these interrelationships, love acts as a medium for the exchange of feelings, of information, between individuals. This is truly a case of McLuhan's expression "the medium is the message." The computer has a very definite role to play in the realm of love. Its capabilities for storing, processing, and retrieving information and implementing its prompt transmission can be of paramount importance in creating better communications between organizations, between groups, and between nations, in helping them weld themselves with bonds of love, for no other medium is as effective as love.

"Love," wrote Thoreau, "is the wind, the tide, the waves, the sunshine, its power is incalculable; it is many horsepower. It never ceases, it never slacks; it can move the globe without a resting place; it can warm without fire; it can feed without meat; it can clothe without garments; it can shelter without roof; it can make a paradise within which will dispense with a paradise without. But though the wisest men in all ages have labored to publish this force, and every human heart is, sooner or later, more or less, made to feel it, yet how little is actually applied to social ends."

"Yet how little is actually applied to social ends." How little, indeed! "Love" is not a respectable idea among scientists and technologists, and, so far as they are concerned, has no connection whatever with the work in which they are engaged. But this is only a measure of the distance that now separates men from the understanding of the purpose for which they exist. It has been said that purposes are born, not made. That may to a large extent be true, but what the statement ignores is man's peculiar evolutionary history, which emphasizes what the great American mathematician and philosopher Charles Sanders Peirce called "evolutionary love." This love constitutes an inbuilt value system that strives for realization in every human being within the bosom of a loving family, even if that family consists of the mother alone in interaction with her child.

Because he was much more than a mathematician, Peirce saw, as he wrote, that ". . . growth comes only from love . . . from the ardent impulse to fulfill another's highest impulse." Even for ideas, "It is not by dealing out cold justice to the circle of my ideas that I can make them grow, but by cherishing and tending them as I would flowers in my garden. . . . Love recognizing germs of loveliness in the hateful, gradually warms it into life, and makes it lovely." Peirce was one of the few scientists of his day, or for the matter of that of any other day, who saw love not only as a factor of evolution but as a primary force in social life. His essay "Evolutionary Love," published in *The Monist* in January 1893, is very much still worth reading.[1] No society can endure without love as its prime mover; unless man realizes this in time and does what is required, his extinction is only a matter of time.

Some readers may wonder why so much attention is given to love in a book devoted to the effects of the computer upon mankind. The answer is that love plays a paramount role in human affairs, one we must understand if we are to achieve the full stature of our humanity—and the computer is the tool that can help us accomplish this understanding. There is a cybernetic linkage between love and knowledge. Love becomes more powerful when better understood, while knowledge becomes more potent—and the computer, with its powers and capabilities, is the basic tool that can help bring it all about. The key to understanding human nature is the necessity for love in the growth and development of the individual and society. This is not a theory, but a fact, and a fact constitutes a verified theory.[2]

THE ROLE OF LOVE

Because of his unique evolutionary history, his loss of instincts, his increased educability, his long period of dependency, his growth in interdependency, man needs to give and receive. This need stands at the very center of all the basic needs, those that must be satisfied if the organism is to survive physically. Love stands like the central sun around which the planets in their orbits revolve. Love is the supreme need that must be satisfied if the organism is to develop as a healthy human being—that is, one who is able to love, to work, and to play.

Whatever man's evolutionary destiny, he will largely make it

---

[1] Reprinted in Charles S. Peirce, *Chance, Love, and Logic* (New York: George Braziller, 1956), pp. 267-300.

[2] For a development of these ideas, see Ashley Montagu, *The Direction of Human Development*, rev. ed. (New York: Hawthorn Books, 1970); Ashley Montagu, *On Being Human*, 2d ed. (New York: Hawthorn Books, 1967); and Ashley Montagu, *The Human Revolution* (New York: Bantam Books, 1967).

himself. That destiny can best be realized if man follows his built-in value system, a system that makes love supreme. Steering his course by the compass of his built-in value system, man may bring about a happier life than has ever been known on this earth. That is an achievable ideal worth working for, one in which the computer can be a major instrument to bring it about.

Because human nature is infinitely malleable, human beings can be tailored to fit almost any desired pattern. Man is custom-made, and custom is king. But although monarchy is not yet altogether outmoded in the world, it has been replaced by more efficient forms of government in some lands. Customs, like kings, can be changed, and should be changed when they have outlived their usefulness. Here, too, the computer can serve, because it can provide an almost continuous reexamination of the validity of "first principles" and other ideas that have become orthodoxies. This would possibly re-semble a giant perpetual vectorial analysis in a multidimensional system in which every possible relevant variable would be holisti-cally evaluated to indicate needed modifications. Thus all complex variables that characterize a working society would be fully up to date and synchronized. Social change under such conditions would flow virtually automatically, although completely under man's con-trol, and no aspect of the culture would lag behind the whole. What is being developed here is not the theme of the manner in which human nature can be computerized, but rather of the way in which the computer can serve in the optimum development and fulfillment of individual human beings.

We need, of course, to explore human nature further, its poten-tial and its possibilities, its structure and its limitations, all as they function in relation to the individual, the social group, and the com-munity of man. This is fundamental for the guidance and control of man's adaptation to his fellow man and to the biosphere in which he lives.

THE COMPUTER AND MAN'S FUTURE

It has been said that the more opportunities are maximized, the more education people are offered, and the more available the computer becomes for such purposes, the more alike people will become. Noth-ing could be further from the truth.

As an information-processing system, every individual, as he grows and develops, undergoes unique experiences that, as information, he selects, transmits, and stores in individual ways. Experiencing the world, and remembering what he has experienced, the individual processes information more and more by feedback of what he has earlier experienced. Thus he becomes even more different from everyone and everything else on earth.

Greater opportunities and education will stimulate the development of these differences among individuals. While individuals will effectively be more alike in their humanity, in the art and science of their humanity, in their abilities and interests, and in the combinations of these, they will differ very widely. It is in the combination of individuals, and the diversity of these abilities and interests they hold in common, that the great human wealth of humanity lies. Computers will make possible the full use of these riches for the benefit of all.

The computer can hold secure the future against the shortsightedness of the past. Foresight is the last of the gifts granted by the gods to man. It has also been said that where there is no vision, the people perish (*Proverbs*). Who, looking back on his life and on the life of humanity, can doubt the wisdom of these apothegms? But men forget or too late recollect the wisdom of their forefathers. Computers will alter all of that.

With the wider introduction of computers into every aspect of human society, the energies of man will be, for the first time, efficiently and economically used. The loss of the wisdom and knowledge of earlier generations will be a thing of the past. Computerized, it will always be available to us for our guidance and enlightenment. Man will have acquired not merely a faithful, immortal memory, but also a means of accelerating and regulating the quality of his own development. Thus he will for the first time be able to test the foundations of his beliefs and chart the course of his future development.

Man stands between the old and the new worlds. How he steps into the new world will largely influence what he will become, for man now stands on the threshold of an age unlike any in the past. With the capabilities of the computer available to us, we can reexamine and thoroughly overhaul our basic values and institutions. The values and institutions of early urban man are no longer the requirement of a humanity that, contrary to most visible trends, is more than ever tending to merge into the Family of Man.

LOVE AND THE FUTURE OF MAN

Let us define our terms. Definitions, of course, can be meaningful only at the end rather than the beginning of an inquiry. But, although the inquiry into the nature of man is not yet complete, we know enough today to be able to define it operationally, and we can test and check our statements by the measure of the verifiable facts.

Whatever confers survival benefits in a creatively enlarging manner upon the individual contributes to the welfare of humanity, as a whole, as groups, or as individuals. Operationally this means that each person conducts himself in such a manner toward others as to enable them not only to live but, in living, to be more fully realized, more fully fulfilled, than they would otherwise have been in the absence of such conduct.

This, in fact, is a short description of the meaning of love. It is a very simple statement, and it is a fundamental one. It provides a test by which the individual can determine whether any contemplated conduct is likely to have either good or evil effects, whether it is right or wrong, desirable or undesirable. If the contemplated conduct is likely to contribute to the welfare of the other, if it is likely to help him to live and realize his potential more completely, then a positive sign may be confidently attached to the answer. If it is likely to have the opposite effect, to diminish either the length or the quality of the other's life, or in any way obstruct his fulfillment, then the conduct may be considered negative.

Because love is the really important concept, we shall use it here as the more effective counterpart of welfare. By *love* we mean behavior that communicates to others one's profound involvement in their welfare, one's deep interest in their fulfillment, because one is aware that to be human is to be in danger. To be in danger because, by virtue of man's unparalleled educability, he is in peril of being taught an immense number of unsound ideas and ways of meeting the challenges of the human environment, including the needs of other human beings. Therefore, whatever else we do, we will not fail the other in the one need, which, more than any other need, he must have satisfied if he is to become a healthy human being. We will never commit the supreme treason that most people commit against others—letting them down when they most stand in need of us. But rather, we will be standing by, giving them all the support, all the sustenance, and all the stimulation they require for their growth (increase in dimension) and development (increase in complexity), so that they may become as human beings the same toward us as we are toward them. This is love, the most important of all the experiences that the infant and child must receive if they are to develop as healthy human beings, able to love, to work, and to play. The ability to love, to work, and to play is the definition of mental health.

Loving must be the primary activity of the parents, and especially of the mother. This is what the function of our schools must primarily be, and this is what the meaning of education should be: the science and art of loving. Both the theory (science) and the practice (art) of loving should constitute the primary foundation and meaning of all education, in our schools, colleges, and universities. Unless the human being knows how to love—and the only way one learns to love is by being loved—he will not become a healthy human being, but rather, to the extent that he has been failed in the experience of love, an unhealthy, awkward, confused creature.

Computers, no matter what the original purpose of their design, can evolve to benefit man, to enable him to realize his potential to the fullest, first his potential for love and, second, his potential for conferring survival benefits in a creatively enlarging manner on others. Thus, technology, science, art, literature—all must be viewed as somewhat different approaches to the greater humanization of man. By humanization is meant the ability to respond lovingly and sensitively to all experience, actual or envisioned. Life is not merely existence; it is or should be to live as if to live and love were one. It is not so much the quantity of years lived as the quality we put into the quantity, however brief or long. Longevity without those qualities that distinguish a loving human being from one that merely exists and exploits his environment, far from being a benison, is a curse—for man is worse than nothing unless he is a spiritually developed character. He need not be religious in the sense of churchgoing—for among the churchgoers there have always been some of the most irreligious, bigoted, and spiritually empty people of their time—but in the sense of that awareness of the interconnectedness of all things that bind one to them: of that consciousness of the unity of all nature, and the reverence for life, that the greatest of all man's accomplishments is the art of living, the art of participating in humanity.

There may be more sanctity in a child's learning the multiplication table or how to use a computer than in all the "Amens" in the world, but not if he begins or ends with the multiplication table or the computer. There is much more to sanctity than that. The single-mindlessness with which techniques and skills are pursued in the Western World has shown us all too personally to what disasters such material devotions lead. And yet few call it "mindlessness," for did it not take some of the most technically skilled scientists and technologists, political wizards, and public relations personnel to produce atom and hydrogen bombs, intercontinental ballistic missiles, nerve gas, America's war in Vietnam, not to mention freeways, urban redevelopment, billboards, and so on?

Yes, technically skilled individuals did accomplish these things, but they were not skillful enough to foresee the consequences of their technical skills. What is the use of any invention or discovery if, in the end, it destroys us all? What is the use of any technology if its by-products pollute our waters, poison our air, and lacerate and uglify the land? Very few of our inventors and discoverers foresaw the destructive consequences of the technology they had created. And, if they did, could they, as individuals, have done anything to prevent such occurrences? In some cases, possibly, in most, not; for the control over such matters is exercised, not by individuals, but by the community or the nation. But, since all groups and nations are made up of individuals, what the quality of their decisions will be worth in considering the consequences of any conduct will clearly depend upon the quality of the individuals in the group or nation. That quality must embrace the ability to think holistically, to see the wood for the trees, and to understand what role the wood plays in the economy of nature, and its relation to the rest of the world. This, too, the computer, above all else, will make possible.

It is not enough, magnificent as that is, for the computer to make the necessary information available to men—men must be ready to seek it, and to apply it when it becomes available. Our scientists and technologists, and our teachers, must be trained to think and perceive holistically, instead of in the traditional manner of thinking and perceiving bits and pieces and parts. Fragmented, atomized, partistic thinking has more than once very nearly put a period to the human enterprise.

The abstract in consideration of good intentions is not good enough, and the making of recurrent unilluminating bows to our better selves may be hypocritically satisfying, but it is ultimately discreditably unsatisfying and destructive. Knowledge is not enough, nor is love, but knowledge with love leads to understanding, and that is what we must holistically achieve. A natural cybernetic relationship exists between love and knowledge, the feedback between the two governing the understanding it yields—love controls the use of knowledge and informs it; knowledge makes more powerful the practice of love and the growth of understanding. It is the triad of love/knowledge/understanding that constitutes the three great chords of human power, and the computer must function in the greater service of these.

12

The Computer and the Future of Man

Splendid as are man's many creations, they all share in a common vulnerability. They can be far too easily misused and their powers and potential made to serve evil as well as good with the same effectiveness. This potential that man's creations have to turn back upon their creator has led to the concept of the Ultimate Weapon outlined at the start of Chapter 1. Today, the computer is the Ultimate Weapon among us, and we are faced with the problem of determining how we can combine its powers with our own abilities to use them to the best advantage of humanity.

The problem is an increasingly serious one, for the computer is primarily an information processing device. Traditionally, information was one of man's most precious possessions, one that could guide his future progress and thereby set him free. The computer has immeasurably magnified the value of information, but it has also transformed it into a resource—no longer held in trust for all of mankind, but a commodity that can be used, developed, controlled, and sold. We have not been unwarned concerning this danger. In the very dawn of the computer's history, Norbert Wiener, in his book *The Human Use of Human Beings*,[1] spoke of the dangers that would be caused by

1 (Boston: Houghton Mifflin Co., 1950).

181

selfish exploitation of the computer's potential. This potential has unfolded since then, and the best way that we can guard ourselves against its misuse and use it for the common good is through the application of love—mankind's basic principle and our ultimate safeguard of all of man's public and private activities.

GOVERNMENT—TOWARD THE PARLIAMENT OF MAN

The computer's impact will be felt most directly on our forms of government. This is a certainty, not just a likelihood, because so little has been done by men to bring their governmental systems up to date, and the age of these systems is showing. This applies to everyone alike, to the Communists and their grotesque fancies that they are implementing on earth the best of 19th-century utopian socialism, or to our own illusions that we are still living in Jefferson's Republic (and, reading history, one might wonder why it should be so admired).

The United States has been in business as a democracy longer than any other important nation, and the antiquity of its institutions is therefore the more readily apparent. Our voting procedures are still primitive (efforts to computerize them have so far proven utter failures, with programming errors largely to blame), and inasmuch as voting is not compulsory, the number of actual voters may well depend on the weather or on the availability of competing attractions (few elections are held during the baseball season). Few citizens actually participate at the grass-roots level in the selection and support of candidates for office and in the surveillance of all government actions. In government itself, expert opinion is often disregarded while demagoguery is the rule. There have been frequent criticisms of the practice of holding national elections every four years for the president and for other fixed terms for legislators. Instead, many say, an administration's tenure should be governed more by the will and satisfaction of the people than by the length of its term of office. This is already the case in most parliamentary democracies where the party in power is always subject to recall and new elections.

Thomas Jefferson called the presidency of the United States "this splendid misery." The term "misery" becomes increasingly accurate, even though the splendor is wearing off, as the weight of decision placed in one man's hands becomes unbearably heavy. The incumbent is from the start crushed by complexity—in matters of domestic and foreign policy—and in matters of technology, which are becoming vital at home and abroad, but which he is equipped neither to understand nor to resolve. To aid him, he has assistants who are either political appointees whose dependability may come into question, and an immense bureaucracy that often seems more like a thick barrier to frustrate his will than an orderly structure responsive to his instructions.

The inefficiency and waste, featherbedding, boondoggling, and corruption that result under our present system often reach Brobdingnagian proportions. The situation is further complicated by the federal structure. The existence of states makes it far easier to govern the separate areas of the nation and serve their very different needs than it is to govern the nation as a whole. However, the differences in their respective laws and constitutions can reach extremes that bring added complication to the government of the nation. In such a system, the individual citizen may feel more like a victim than like a participating member of his society. He plays no role in decision making. Others decide, and all that he can do is to abide by the decision and pay for the privilege. He does not even select the candidates for whom he is expected to vote. Isolation, anonymity, impersonality, and the fragmentation of the social order, all contribute to the citizenry's feelings of helplessness and impotence that have become so pervasive in our society today.

The computer will have a powerful impact on our political dishevelment. Through its agency, we will be able to cope with many problems that have been too long outstanding (though it may be at the price of creating new issues for the future). This will be chiefly because of the advances in the feasibility and economy of information collection and dissemination that will be made possible through the use of computerized systems.

Today, information about our government, about the candidates who ask us to elect them, and about how they perform once they are elected, is the exclusive property of a very few organizations—newspapers, radio and television networks, wire services, and a limited number of magazines. We have to accept what information they care to or decide to give us. They have little incentive to give us better information owing to competition because the cost of creating communications media is still so high that they represent near monopolies. This cost, however, is now starting to go down rapidly, and it will become increasingly economical for the new media to aim their messages at selected groups, limited in size rather than at mass audiences. Cable television, for instance, may make it possible to broadcast to selected neighborhoods at a cost far lower than that of using today's metropolitan newspapers or broadcasting stations. There will thus be a wealth of information much more readily available to very special interest groups.

Most people do not belong to well-defined groups and are thus unlikely to accept any group-oriented message without questions. Answering these questions without excessive cost and effort would often be impractical today. In the future, however, it is widely expected that most homes will be equipped with data terminals, providing instant access to central computer data banks that can at slight cost process information or retrieve and edit it for the inquirer, whether office worker or housewife. The growing availability of these terminals and of specialized communications will undoubtedly increase the political sophistication of the electorate. It will also make it possible for individual voters to obtain from the data banks more detailed and significant information concerning candidates and issues before deciding their vote.

Yet a third aspect of the computer's impact, and one that is still almost impossible to evaluate, is the far greater equality of opportunity that will exist among all political parties and factions as the cost of access to communications media declines precipitously. Currently, the leaderships of many political organizations keep a tight grip on their candidates through control of campaign funds. In the future, this control will be negated and individual candidates will be far freer to take stands in which they wholeheartedly believe. Certainly, this will erode the existing two-party system, and open the way for far greater political complexity. One way in which this complexity may be solved will be through direct consultation of the entire population on important issues. The home data terminals will be readily usable for this purpose. It would be impractical to hold daily national consultations on the routine affairs of the government. However, there will more and more frequently be instances (as in the French Fifth Republic) where the nation will have a chance to make its will effectively known before it is committed by its government to a course of action from which there is no return.

The computer will also hasten the decline of bureaucracy. Traditional bureaucracy is a paperwork factory, staffed by armies of secretaries, filing clerks, and numerous other workers, all occupied in generating, classifying, conveying, monitoring, and performing other mysterious operations on vast volumes of records and documents. This paperwork was needed in the past when there was no other means of recording what had happened. It was a lesser evil than the complete chaos that would have reigned without documents. The computer provides an efficient, economical means of storing, processing, and retrieving this information with a minimum of human intervention. In addition, it now becomes possible to institute "management by exception procedure," under which the only things that are done are those that the computer spots as needing to be done.

Computerization of the bureaucratic process will free the bureaucrats, many of whom are competent, motivated individuals, from much of their record-keeping burden and permit them instead to engage in actual administration, decision making, and other activities required for active support of the workings of society. The results for the citizenry will be remarkable. The latter will at last be able to expect and receive prompt and effective responses to their needs and inquiries.

Law, too, will be modified by the computer. Already, it is being used to make courts of law more efficient. Court dockets are being revised by computers to allow for the hearing of more cases in the same length of time. Defense lawyers are using the computer's information processing powers to find legal precedents and organize their evidence, and so are prosecutors. One system, now in operation, allows the local prosecutor's office to estimate its chances of winning particular cases so that it may decide whether or not to prosecute. The computer is also serving and will continue to serve as a powerful tool with which to liberate judges for their real task—that of making decisions requiring individual attention and complete impartiality and equity.

INDUSTRY AND COMMERCE—
MORE BREAKS FOR THE CONSUMER

A society, like ours, that is constantly involved in rapid and unexpected processes of change—and, indeed, depends upon them for its progress—must rely on the computer for basic support. This support has helped human society to develop, through industrialization and worldwide communications, the most complex systems for the integration and orientation of knowledge, attitudes, values, and norms. Yet, despite all that, society is hardly conscious of itself, of its problems, or of its almost unlimited power to deal with those problems. Computers made the landing of men on the moon possible. They can also make the landing of men on earth possible—that is, the healthier realization of man's potentialities on earth.

Computers, as we all know, have become basic tools of industry. They can be and are used to design, manufacture, and quantify anything that needs to be. They are used to design factories or workers' housing, or to supervise the smoothness of vast manufacturing or processing operations, and they do so with the same effectiveness as that with which they serve in the front-office to handle the bookkeeping and accounting work load of the company or factory. Computerized factories employing only a few technicians are becoming ever more common. The day is coming when the relatively unskilled blue-collar worker will belong to the "horse-and-buggy" (early computer) days of the 1960s and 1970s. There will, however, be even more jobs created as a result of the higher incomes that will be made possible by automation and that will cause the creation of ever greater appetites for services. Air travel is an example; the airlines would be hard put today to do without computers. They are used to back up worldwide reservation systems that check on the availability of seats on any flight anywhere, store reservation information and update it, if need be, and are always ready to prepare the actual documents when they are called for. Similarly, they help direct air traffic control, and without them it would be difficult to direct traffic over big city airports on foggy days when planes must wait in stacks trying not to collide with each other as they circle in their tight holding patterns.

Some of the chief and best breaks, however, will in the future go to the consumer. Knowing what the best buy is, is an increasingly difficult accomplishment for the average shopper, bedeviled by diversity and the difficulties of suburban travel. Computerized centers will provide comparative product evaluations, much like *Consumer Reports* has been doing for many years, and give detailed descriptions of available features. Consumers will thus be able to obtain prompt and up-to-date action information on which to base their shopping decisions.

Additional support will come to the consumer in the future through the development of electronic shopping services. Would-be buyers will be shown, through their home data and television terminals, pictures of, and given information concerning, the items available in the class of products that they want. This information will also include the store where they are sold, and the customer will be able, if he or she desires, to purchase the item for delivery through the home terminal. The same transaction will include an authorization for the payment to be debited directly and instantly from the customer's bank balance. Thanks to the computer, individual consumers will be able to save much time that would otherwise be devoted to the routine tasks of daily survival, and they will thus be able to devote more time to their careers, their families, or to their further self-improvement.

EDUCATION—THE MEANINGS BEHIND THE FACTS

The ideal of education for all has been very nearly achieved in this century. Now the computer will make possible individualized education for everyone—to enable each individual to realize his uniqueness, to educate and fulfill himself so that he, in turn, can educate and stimulate others. Teachers will thus be liberated from the Sisyphean labor of drilling, repeating, and grading. The student will be liberated from the rote learning of facts. He will learn that education is a creative process, *not* an engorge-and-disgorge performance. Depersonalized education as we know it will become a horrid curiosity belonging to the Dark Ages of society.

Education is not a process of accumulating knowledge, but the process of learning how to bring about creative changes in the continuum of experience. It is not a process of accumulation, but one of transformation in which the learner learns to transform creatively. This process of transformation can be applied even to education itself, using the computer-related technique of systems analysis. Systems analysis can be used to examine and evaluate nearly all aspects of the educational environment, starting with the design of school programs; the validity of current and proposed curricula and teaching methods; and the behavior, performance, and interrelationships of the faculty, the students, and the community.

Systems analysis is a masterful tool for decision making. Its use can involve the skill of several experts, sometimes a considerable number, in various disciplines to analyze every possible relevant set of interrelated activities. The comprehensiveness and flexibility of the decisions thus arrived at allow the planning of educational and other programs with far greater effectiveness than could previously be achieved. This is reflected in the growing use that is being made of systems analysis in educational planning projects.[2]

Because the computer will reduce by millions the persons necessary to do the work that formerly could be done only by human beings, the working day and week will be greatly shortened. The result will be more freedom and leisure for more people than human beings have ever enjoyed. We rejoice in the prospect, but we must be forewarned and plan for the problems that freedom and leisure on such a scale will inevitably cause.

Freedom and leisure are gifts we must be properly prepared to use, or they will be abused. It is here that education, soundly conceived, must assume its proper role. The computer can plan educational programs through which everyone will be enabled to find greater enjoyment in the increasing opportunities for leisure.

It may be true that the computer will never fully replace the human teacher in the classroom; in any event, we think it undesirable. Teaching begins with caring for those who are to be taught. Although it might be possible to communicate caring through a computer, the student would be unable to relate and respond to a machine. Of course, there are human teachers who cannot relate to students and to whom in turn students cannot relate, but such "teachers" do not belong in a classroom.

In the future the computer can be of the greatest assistance in selecting those who are competent to teach and reject those—no matter what their academic qualifications may be—who are not competent to teach. Such selection might even begin when application is made for admission to teachers colleges and other institutions that train teachers.

The student must learn skills, techniques, attitudes, values, knowledge, understanding, and, above all, love. Of these seven educational objectives, the last two, understanding and love, can be taught only in the interactive social process between an understanding, loving teacher and student. The care of the learner begins with caring for the learner. On this fundamental level, then, the computer cannot replace teachers.

However, the computer can help the student deepen his understanding of the meaning and significance of love. The computer can

<hr>

[2] See John Pfeiffer, *New Look at Education* (New York: The Odyssey Press, 1968).

be questioned on such matters as "What does one mean when one speaks of a mother loving her child? How, if at all, does this differ from the same mother when she says she loves her husband, her parents, her siblings?" "What relation has love of country to 'falling in love'?" "How many kinds of love are there?" "Are violence and love always incompatible?" "Under what, if any, circumstances is a violent act permissible?" These, and innumerable similar questions can be asked a properly programmed computer, to initiate a dialogue with the machine that will help the student reach appropriate answers. These can then be used for further discussion in the classroom. The same, of course, can be done with all subjects. The computer, however, is no shortcut to the acquisition of values. A computer can provide an immediate answer to a simple problem or even to a complex one, but it cannot serve as a substitute for the direct experience of a value.

As a learning aid, the computer will probably remain for centuries the greatest advance in educational methodology since the invention of the alphabet. The computer can place the learning process under the individual control of the student. No longer will he be the anonymous part of an agglutinated mass of learners omeletted all together in the classroom, all exposed to the same learning experience, and all expected to learn in depth and breadth at the same rate. Instead, each learner will be treated as an individual with his own learning rate, his own interests, his own capabilities, and his own motivations.

In the classroom, each student, at elementary and secondary school, will have his own console with television screen. He will receive the attention of the computer, no matter where he may be in the course, and no matter on what subject he may be concentrating. The computer will enable each student to receive individual attention consonant with his particular needs. Since the computer can remember the problems and weaknesses as well as strengths of the student in prior performances, no advance will be made until the student has mastered every step in learning the subject. Here the computer may be able to do what the teacher cannot; that is, supervise the practice and repetition necessary for each individual student to master a subject, skill, or technique.

The computer will make many examinations obsolete, since no student can complete a computerized course until he has mastered every step. The need for periodic or final examinations is thus obviated. Furthermore, since it has been shown that students learn more efficiently at the computer, as well as three to four times more rapidly than by conventional methods, students will be able to learn a great deal more in a shorter period of time than by traditional methods.

The lecture has long been something of an anachronism. It was the only method of teaching until the invention of printing. As a method of teaching it is already declining, and will be resorted to only when necessary. The material that was formerly delivered in lecture form can now be received by students on a variety of instruments. The computer will also counsel the student on personal matters.

It has been found that autistic children, who exhibit extreme withdrawal, relate much more effectively to a computer than they do to human beings; and likewise it will be found that students will more frankly present their problems to a computer than to another person.

At the college and university levels, the computer will become a teaching and learning tool of major importance. It not only will increase the knowledge and understanding of techniques, skills, and human relations, but will be applied to the problems of society at every level—social, ideological, political, technological, scientific, and so on. In this manner, community, university, students, and teachers will form a large integrated community, instead of being separated as for the most part they still are, into "Town" and "Gown," "Faculty" and "Students."

In the Age of the Computer, working together for the common good will be the new style, and the old style, prevailing today, will be thought of as the Stone Age of education.

The new style will emphasize the original meaning of the word "education," "to care, to nourish, to cause to grow," from the Latin *educare*. Anglicizing the pronunciation of the word emphasizes its real meaning—the development of the ability to care for others. The emphasis on the "caring" is the missing principle the new education will restore to humanity. Thus, for the first time in man's history will an effective means, the computer, be joined to a visionary dream: the achievement of a genuine civilization of humanity. H.G. Wells once characterized human history as a race between education and catastrophe; with the computer's help, the race will have been won—by education.

PREPARING FOR LEISURE

Freeing man from the curse of Adam, the computer will not automatically lead to man's using his leisure to improve himself. It would more likely lead to his corruption and the corrosion of his soul. Man should be physically and mentally fit for retirement, and no one should retire until he is adequately prepared to assume the obligations and responsibilities of retirement. No man should be presented with the gift of leisure without first being educated to use it. Hence, much planning will be necessary before the computer automates so much of the world's work that men now do. Television, radio, motion pictures, and "sports" are no substitute for the intelligent use of leisure. On the contrary, these media, a good deal of the time, enable one to evade those tasks, enjoyments, and relaxations, for which the prepared mind is eager.

Without denying the value of occasionally doing nothing or wasting time, most leisure time should be used creatively. In other words, leisure should be a time not only for relaxation, but for doing things with the family—reading, writing, visiting friends, museums, art galleries, attending concerts, the theater, working at one's hobbies, and so on. Leisure makes work a pleasure because it is work that one chooses. And such work is best done because it is freely chosen and pleasurable. Labor that one is obliged to do will collectively consume no more than a few months of the year, and there will be no more debasing and degrading labor. Work will assume entirely new qualities, for it will largely be the activity of one's leisure time, it being understood that work is the activity one enjoys, and labor the activity that is obligatory, and that one may or may not enjoy, but will not detest. Leisure will also change from a time when one relaxes or escapes to a time when one works creatively for personal and collective fulfillment. It will differ greatly from the erosive leisure so widely prevalent today.

Disraeli once remarked that increased means and increased leisure are the two civilizers of man, but only, of course, if they are intelligently and creatively used; otherwise, they can be a misfortune. Leisure alone does not automatically lead to the refinement of humanity. The joyless and uncreative pursuit of pleasure and the mindless vulgarities that pass for "amusement" by so many are proof of that.

The problem of leisure can be solved, we believe, through education. Education will make explicit the choices between opting for the best or settling for the indifferent or the worst, in a community in which the leaders offer the best they can give rather than what they think the people want. Man must be prepared for leisure long before the Computer Age becomes fully established. That time is imminent. We see little attempt to plan for it. The opportunity is now. It will make all the difference in the world whether we take advantage of it now or not.

APPLICATIONS IN THE HOME

The computer will serve individuals, not only as consumers, but also as direct users of the information-processing and retrieval services, which are the computer's primary products. The role for the individual will not be limited only to searching catalogs and other lists for desired products, and, through the terminal console, reporting on their availability. The computer can also be used as a reminder or service for all engagements, dates, appointments, and the like, the reminders appearing automatically, several times at definite intervals.

The computer will also maintain home accounts, and all other types of accounts. Income tax, kept continuously up to date, on the basis of the cumulative records of income, deductions, contributions, and expenses, will be automatically prepared on a quarterly and annual schedule, well ahead of the due time.

Information on any subject—current events, weather predictions, stock-market returns, sports events, critics' views of movies, plays, and exhibitions, and so on—will be available almost instantly. Similarly, anything in print—a line, a paragraph, a page, a whole book, a newspaper or magazine—will be immediately at hand. Not only citizens, but researchers, scholars, technologists, industrialists, and many others will find the availability of information a great boon. Not only can a complete bibliography or reference list be made available, but also a selective rundown of what the particular inquirer is likely to find most relevant—according to his stated interests. The central computer will transmit whatever material the inquirer requires either verbatim or in digest form. The convenience of such a service and the time it will save will be tremendous.

In short, the citizen at home with his console will have the whole world of information literally at his fingertips. Not only this, he will have information available to him that will fit whatever special needs he has. His chief problem will be to formulate his requests for data in such a way that he can be reasonably certain of receiving the best answers to his questions.

He will be able to sit at home, and if he or any member of the family feels unwell, he can transmit the symptoms through linked instruments to get back a list of possible ailments and a differential diagnosis that will enable him then to determine what needs to be done next, including simple home medication if no physician is required.

His house can be run automatically by computer, when he is both home and away. Thus, all electrical and gas appliances can be turned off automatically, windows closed when it begins to rain, and opened again when the rain ceases. Temperature and humidity can be automatically controlled, automobile engines warmed up in damp or cold weather before they are to be used, and, indeed, all transportation, particularly automobiles, can be automated. Some automated automobiles have already passed the experimental stages. In time, the catastrophic pressures of automobile traffic may compel the use of computers to control traffic and automobiles.

THE EFFECTS OF THE COMPUTER UPON MANKIND

Because it processes information rapidly, the computer will turn the earth into a great global village. Satellites and computers not only will make weather prediction universal and accurate, but will bring every and any happening to anyone who wishes to know of it as it is occurring. This will, perhaps, serve to unify mankind where all else has failed.

When human beings are in touch with one another, share common interests in the village, continent, or globe, they are likely to become concerned and involved. It is when people are separated that they come to regard each other as foreign, different, and opposed. Familiarity, on the other hand, shows us that under all the superficial differences, human beings are alike. Their interests are best realized not in opposition, hostility, or conflict, but by understanding, cooperation, and love. Narrow nationalisms will end, and the human world will become one great extended family, with brothers, and sisters, and cousins in every land. Taking the likenesses for granted, we shall also accept the physical and cultural differences as the common heritage of all humanity, just as we accept the individual differences in members of the same family as part of the heritage of that family. These differences will enrich human lives, for they offer such varied ways of experiencing the world that individual and community life will take on new dimensions of understanding.

The potentialities for humanity of every baby form an inheritance that has to be carefully nurtured if it is to become a living creative power. In that sense, its only really meaningful sense, humanity is not an inheritance but an achievement. It is both a collective and an individual achievement, in which those who turn the child into a humane being help him also to continue the process for himself. In this process the child, in addition to learning from its everyday experience, will be able to ask questions of its computer whenever it wishes, and thus further enable it to enlarge its competence in human relations. Use of the computer will, of course, be taught in elementary and secondary schools.

Every culture, every society, represents man's development in adjusting to his environment, and achieving some control over it. Before the 20th century, that environment was usually limited in scope. Today, however, the boundaries are dissolving and mankind is moving—in spite of occasional appearances to the contrary—toward unity without uniformity, toward the condition in which the differences that now separate men will grow to be regarded, not with fear, suspicion, and discrimination, but as we have already said, as unimportant as the differences among the members of the same family.

As Norbert Wiener, the Father of Cybernetics put it, the community extends only so far as there extends an effectual transmission of information.[3] This means that information must be shared or is so readily available that it can be shared upon request. No one, of course, will ever be able to be in individual possession of all information, but it should be readily available to everyone, and socially shared.

The easy availability of information will greatly contribute to individual development, in a world in which the community, the nation, the state, exist for the individual who, in turn, encourages the development of all other individuals—not that the individual exists

[3] Norbert Wiener, *Cybernetics* (New York: John Wiley & Sons, 1948), p. 184.

for the community (or the state or the world), but that both reciprocally exist for each other. Some individuals will be wiser than the community and the computer, and some will not. In our new world, wisdom, invention, and discovery will increase, and unwisdom will be reduced.

Are these exaggerated expectations? False hopes based on an optimistic view of man and his nature? They most certainly are if we believe that the computer simply by computing will solve all our problems. The computer unassisted by men of goodwill certainly cannot solve man's problems. Fundamentally, computers will never be any more humane than the human beings who program them. Hence, we shall always need built-in devices to protect the individual and the community against any misuses of the computer for selfish ends. Such devices should not be too difficult to develop, and will probably always be necessary.

THE COMPUTER AND POPULATION CONTROL

At the present time there are too many people in the world—3.75 billion. By the end of this century there will be, if man goes on reproducing at his present rate, double that number, with results that can only be described as catastrophic. Foreseeing this, this cataclysmic growth of population could be prevented. And here, too, the computer can play its part.

Overpopulation is not so much a problem of quantity as of quality. Quantity debases quality. There will not be enough food to feed everyone in the world, but even if there were, that is not the issue at stake. The issue at stake is whether human beings should proliferate so irresponsibly that they deprive both themselves, their children, and others of self-fulfillment and self-realization. In short, overpopulation effectively prevents millions upon millions of individuals from ever realizing their potentialities even at a minimum level. It creates poverty, social disorganization, normlessness, disengagement, crime, and political strife. It is the world's priority problem, and unless it is solved, no other social problem can be solved.

The computer can help us solve the population problem by providing answers to the specific problems of each community on an international basis. Computers can provide the answers, but governments must implement them. The great advances in population control have come from private agencies, almost invariably in conflict with existing mores and governmental sanctions. The prosecution and trials of Annie Besant, Charles Bradlaugh, and Margaret Sanger, not to mention numerous others in our own day, testify to the resistance of entrenched institutions and the shortsightedness of human beings, to selfless endeavors of such men and women to improve the conditions and quality of human life. Because of the courageous and pioneering labors of such splendid human beings, some effective methods of birth control now exist, and abortion is legal in some states; so advances have been made, and continue to be made. Our failure in India, however, where one million babies are added each month to an already oversized population of 600 million, after 25 years of attempting to teach birth control, has shown us that only full-scale schemes, having complete governmental backing, as in Japan, can possibly succeed in the control of population growth.

This matter is urgent. Few governments seem concerned with controlling population; yet failure to act will be disastrous. An M.I.T. group, working on a continuing "Project on the Predicament of Mankind," has constructed computer models of the future using a variety of assumptions. According to Dr. Dennis Meadows, of M.I.T.'s Alfred P. Sloane School of Management, their preliminary models show that if current trends are not reversed, population will decline between 50 and 80 percent during the 21st century. By then, however, the population at present rates of increase will have reached the staggering number of 48 billion. All resource experts believe that the earth could not possibly support that many people. An age of unprecedented bleakness would descend upon the world long before such a number was reached. The computer can help avoid this grim prospect.

NEW HOPE FOR URBAN DWELLERS

The city is associated with the rise of civilized life—and so it should continue to be, but not in its present disastrous form. The contemporary city is a disaster because its growth was unplanned and uncontrolled. Overcrowded, overpopulated, slum-ridden, traffic-congested, polluted, uglified, and dehumanized, the city is no longer habitable. To become livable again, the city must be radically changed. Volumes have been written on this subject and innumerable designs for new cities have been proposed. Some of these designs have even been executed, and in most cases only worsened conditions. "Urban renewal" has become the euphemism for traumatic displacement—the replacement of the community by high-rise cave dwellings. In housing redevelopment, more homes and houses are destroyed than are ever again made available.

Today's designers of cities quite obviously dislike the old, and many dislike cities altogether, and hence design anticities. Many new city designers do not seem to understand that a city is for living, growing, and developing human beings who live on the ground and not in the skies. While human beings enjoy privacy, they are also social beings who enjoy being with others. The city should maximize rather than reduce the opportunities for community interaction.

"Middle-income housing," as it is disingenuously called, constitutes the most depressing example of a failure to understand human need. Such projects only too often resemble barracks that segregate increasingly larger numbers of people from each other. Is this the best that our designers and planners can do? Is this a fair view of the future? Must every building be known by a letter of the alphabet and/or a number? Must the residents follow signs to their own apartment, to the cave with all the "conveniences" of modern life and not a single contribution to that contentment that can only come from the sense of community.

The tremendous technological advances of the 19th and 20th centuries have made large cities anachronistic. Once, large cities needed many people to make them run. People lived where often they could walk or take horse-drawn public transportation to work. Suburbs as we know them did not exist. The corner grocery store, the baker, the shoemaker, the candy store, the church, the school, and the family doctor could all be reached by walking. Each community was a vital center for its members. Grandparents, sons and daughters, grandchildren, and their relatives, lived near one another; the extended family flourished and was part of a tightly knit community.

The vital center is gone now with the corner store. The community no longer exists, and the extended family is dead. Workers who can afford it have moved out of the cities and reenter only to work or visit a theater or dine. But for the rest, the city is a place from which to escape. The streetcar has been replaced by the inefficient bus, and public transit more and more by the automobile, which seems to have wreaked more havoc than any other invention of man. The automobile enables man to live in the suburbs while working in the city. This ultimately saps the economic life of the city, leaving the downtown business and industry to wither away. The inner city begins to deteriorate, and unemployment and poverty rise. The city's finances are drained by the millions poured out in relief and the decaying streets and houses, the police force, crime control, not to mention the huge sums paid to consultants to find solutions to problems that under the prevailing conditions are essentially insoluble. The counsel of the consultants is therefore generally ignored.

The megalopolis is a socially pathological development that shortsighted planners have foreseen as a solution to the problems of the city. The truth is that giganticizing the city will only make its problems even more complex than they already are. It is the small town rather than the gigantic city that is more likely to solve the problems of contemporary city life. The large city is neither manageable, liveable, nor governable—as we may judge from what has been happening to such cities as Newark, New York, Detroit, Cleveland, and many others. The city can no longer serve the purposes that originally brought it into being. It has, indeed, long outlived its usefulness as a place for people to live in. The cities are increasingly being abandoned to those who cannot afford to leave them, and who live in the ghettos, while the rich, who can afford to remain, live in the cliff dwellings they call their homes in the "fashionable" parts of town. But, as a community, the city no longer exists, and anyone who complains of the alienation, the indifference, the disengagement, and the rudeness that characterize city inhabitants and city workers is simply underscoring the breakdown of the city and the death of community.

The city has become a wilderness in which human beings lose their humanity because inhumanity has become the way of life of the city—indifference, disengagement, and isolation. What is clearly indicated is not a return to the primitive, but a restoration of men to the life of humanity, of community. This will take a great deal of thought and planning, and in this work the computer will play a principal role. New towns will be developed, and under the conditions of life in those towns, the extended family will once more bring its benefits to humanity.

What is needed are carefully designed new cities, not exceeding a maximum population of 250,000, each with its districts of

25,000 people, with open spaces, beautiful squares, and all the amenities for cooperative living. Countryside should surround each city. Each city should have gardens, with opportunities for residents to cultivate every form of plant life: flowers, fruit trees, and kitchen gardens.

Man must return to the concept of nature as a whole because he is a creature of nature who, in civilized societies, has domesticated himself. Urban man especially lives under highly artificial conditions, in most cases isolated from nature. Many such city dwellers have never seen an apple on a tree and animals other than domestic ones or those in zoos. This virtually complete separation from nature leads to a view of it that is wholly 'disengaged, even alienated, and frequently hostile. This is a pathological state, a morbid dissociation from what should always have remained a vital involvement with nature.

Man's several million years of evolution spent in close interrelationship with nature helped to form him and make possible everything he has since done. We believe, with Benjamin Rush, that "Man is naturally a wild animal . . . taken from the woods he is never happy . . . till he returns to them again." This does not mean that an archetypal species of memory exists, but it does mean that man is a part of nature, and that his relation to it is not merely one of natural harmony and ecologic necessity, but also of civilized health. Detachment from nature results in impoverishment of the spirit. Most city dwellers feel this, and hence the strong urge that often comes upon them to return to the wilderness, to nature. The enormous number of people who enjoy camping out, and even those who prefer more sophisticated reversions to the wilderness, such as a country or seashore hotel, or those "Isles of Illusion" that dot the Caribbean, constitute an illuminating testimony not only to the desire for a change of scene, but to the deep-seated need to get out into the open. As Keats wrote long ago: "To one who has been long in city pent, 'Tis very sweet to look into the fair And open face of heaven. . . ."

To be cut off from nature is to suffer a serious loss and curtailment of life, which the experience, understanding, and appreciation of the wilderness and the kinship with nature and everything in it brings. It is not the notion of nature or the wilderness for their own sake that is of value, but the awareness of one's relatedness to them, one's unity with them, that deepens and extends the scope of human life. The aesthetic life and the enjoyment of the merely picturesque often lead to a sybaritic self-indulgence rather than to spiritual exaltation. And neither the one nor the other is enough, for what is necessary is recognition of the simple fact that our wholeness as human beings depends upon the depth of our awareness of the fact that we are part of the wholeness of nature and that the standards of dominance that we have erected for ourselves in relation to nature are artificial and destructive.

As Immanuel Kant remarked, evolution has been anthropocentrically envisaged as "a very long ladder, created by man to place himself on the highest rung." And so we have created categories of "higher" and "lower" animals, a kind of race prejudice of which the so-called highest may justifiably do with the so-called lowest whatever they opportunistically desire. It is maintained that man is made in God's image, and the beast in the image of the brute. Man, it is further maintained, is loving and intelligent, and therefore superior to all other creatures, who allegedly act from instinct. Many of the learned as well as the ignorant hold such beliefs.

These beliefs are quite unsound, as experience shows. It is written in the Book of Job (12:7):

> Ask now the beasts and they shall teach thee; and the fowls of the air, and they shall tell thee.
> Or speak to the earth, and it shall teach thee; and the fishes of the sea shall declare unto thee.
> Who knoweth not in all these that the hand of the Lord hath wrought this?
> In whose hand is the soul of every living thing, and the breath of all mankind.

And most beautifully it is written in the Koran:

> There is no beast on earth nor fowl that flieth, but the same are a people like unto you, and to God they shall return.

Without necessarily subscribing to these words in their literal sense, the profound truths they express are beyond question, namely, that we can learn from these other "peoples" and that we ought to love and respect them for what they are, our kin. It is the restoration of this sense of kinship that the planning of future human cities can achieve, by making the city a part of the wilderness, and everything that is in it, so that children may know nature as an enriching indispensable part of their lives—where nature is regarded as a beneficent friend and not as an enemy to be subdued and wasted, and where other animals live together as they naturally do, in harmony, a harmony in which man joins.

In planning, building, and designing such cities, the computer will be indispensable, as well as in the continuous maintenance and improvement of them.

CONTROL OF THE ENVIRONMENT

Environmental damage, pollution of the air, sea, lakes, rivers and other bodies of water, the destruction of natural resources, the misuse of pesticides like DDT, are only a few examples of the frightful destruction resulting from the uncontrolled use of, or rather abuse of, nature. Clearly, we must find ways to produce and use energy, dispose of waste, and the like, which will, if not entirely eliminate pollutants, reduce wastes to the barest minimum and at the same time put them to some use. The problems involved are all amenable to computer systems analysis, and every large community should now be using systems analyses toward such ends.

It will, however, not be enough to make such analyses on a state or even national basis, but to be permanently effective they must be undertaken internationally. For example, should South America become highly industrialized, millions of trees would be cut down. The rain forests would be affected, for the timber there is almost unlimited and various. The immediate and long-term results of destroying the forests would be a reduction in the oxygen available not only to the South Americans, but also to the North Americans, for wind carries much rain forest oxygen to North America. This does not mean that without the South American rain forests oxygen will no longer be available for North Americans to breathe, but it does mean that both the amount and quality of oxygen available will be seriously affected. The fact that a single six-cylinder automobile engine running at 30 miles an hour consumes more oxygen in one minute than 25,000 people during the same time should suggest something of the seriousness of the problem.

Systems analysis by computer on a worldwide basis can provide programs for action and effective solutions for every kind of environmental problem. What is needed is an International Environment Board with agencies in every country to oversee world environmental

problems as a whole, and with local and national agencies continuously to monitor and control the environment, man-made and natural. In this manner the world will once more become a healthy habitat
for the whole of animated nature. Not only will the computer be able
to predict the weather weeks and even months ahead, but it will also
be possible to control it by methods that systems analysis by computer will make feasible.

All over the world there are environmental problems of every
kind—agricultural, river control, flooding, land wastage, insect-borne
diseases, poverty—to mention but a few. Direct approaches to solving such problems may not only not prove enough but may, if all the
interrelated possible factors are not taken into consideration, prove
disastrous.

In recent years the possibility of supersonic air transport was discussed. The governments of the United States, France, the U.S.S.R.,
and Britain invested millions of dollars in building a supersonic plane.
The United States withdrew from the project largely owing to public
outrage over the high cost and concern about the noise and vibration
damage resulting from such a plane. But it was not until a study of
the damaging effects upon the atmosphere was made widely known
through the press, television, and radio that Congress finally voted
to discontinue building the plane. A computer systems analysis of
the project and the damaging effects of the plane upon life and environment could have saved money, time, effort, materials, and organization that went into building the SST in the United States.

In as technologically complex a society as ours, all government
projects should first be subjected to a systems analysis. Military
leaders may not respect the intelligence and humanity of intellectuals, but they do respect machinery. If the government and the military had used systems analysis prior to becoming involved, perhaps
millions of human beings dead and injured, a land devastated, and
more than $300 billion lost might have been saved. Perhaps some
day we shall get around to asking computers whether politicians and
generals are really necessary?

By rather clumsy biological means we can determine a child's
sex before it is born. We can determine whether the unborn child has
any of some 80 serious genetic disorders, and in some cases
alleviate or correct such conditions before or immediately after birth.
This constitutes a substantial advance over man's virtually complete
state of ignorance in these matters only a few years ago. The advances

in these areas of knowledge are predictably going to be considerable in the immediate future, and in making those advances possible, computers will play a considerable role.

It would be desirable for every person to be genetically typed. Not only would his blood groups and types be determined but the character also of all his chromosomes. An individual may be the carrier of a defective gene that does not express itself in a disorder in him (in which case it would be said to be carried in the recessive state). Should he have children by a woman carrying the same recessive gene, then the children in whom both genes come together will suffer from the disorder. By examining the chromosomes of the prospective parents or the quantity or quality of various substances in the blood, urine, or certain tissues, it is often possible to determine whether or not the prospective parents are carriers of defective genes, and hence to calculate the risks of their having a child showing the particular genetic disorder. The techniques involved at the present time take several weeks to complete. With the help of computers, the time will be reduced to a minimum.

Ultimately, chromosomal typing (karyotyping) will be performed routinely on every child after birth. Information on every individual's chromosomal, blood, and biochemical traits will already be on record, and through the computer this can be readily available in a matter of moments, to supplement or corroborate the findings made on the particular individuals at later ages. Developing biochemical and other traits can similarly be recorded from time to time and retrieved whenever necessary, together with the evaluation of their significance. In this manner a great many conditions can be noted long before they would otherwise declare themselves, and the proper prophylactic or remedial measures instituted. In fetology (the study of the fetus *in utero*) and in genetics, aided by computers we can expect a massive reduction in the number of defective children born, with a consequent proportionate reduction in the amount of human suffering.

The computer is increasingly being used to monitor the state of well-being of the fetus just before birth, and there can be little doubt that its use will be extended to earlier periods during the fetus' development *in utero*.

At the present time the computer is beginning to be used as an aid in detecting and preventing fetal distress. One device, which monitors fetal heart rate and intrauterine pressure, transmits the data by a tiny radio transmitter. This device requires a doctor or a nurse to be on hand to read the results. A more advanced method lets the computer "listen" to the data, and has it call the human attendants only when they are needed. This is achieved by means of an intra-uterine catheter with a pressure-sensing device that measures the strength of uterine contractions. Electrocardiographic data from the baby is picked up by a tiny clip electrode attached to the presenting part of the baby. These findings are then fed by cable to the monitoring unit, which prints out a running history on graph paper. The data thus obtained is fed to a computer that keeps a 10-minute history of the contractions and heart rate, updated every 3.2 seconds. The graph and the computer can be read and queried at any time to retrieve the history, and if the computer senses anything "wrong," it will immediately signal an attendant.

Such machines, in addition to their "diagnostic" functions are now being developed that would give them decision-making functions that would allow them to control the flow of drugs given to the mother (such as oxytocin, to induce labor), to increase or decrease contractions in order to keep them within normal range.[4]

Using the computer we will be able to draw up a specification of the aptitudes and specific and general intelligence of the growing child, and thus facilitate the optimum development of his abilities by programming social and educational curricula most congenial to his talents and personality. Thus, the computer will make it possible, for the first time in the history of man, to treat the individual as the unique creature he is, and to tailor his social and educational experiences to his needs, instead of, as we have been doing in the past, slighting the uniqueness of the person and treating him as if he were an undifferentiated member of an agglutinated mass.

Similarly, we shall, for the first time, develop medicine for the individual rather than as we practice medicine today, as medicine for the masses. Each individual is psychically as well as physically unique. Although medicine has in the past paid lip service to this notion, the practice of medicine has proceeded on the assumption that every individual is much like every other individual. This is, of course, crudely true—but only crudely. In fact every individual is organically unique, and the computer will diagnose and record such

4"Computer Sounds the Alarm on Problem Childbirths," *Journal of the American Medical Association* 218 (1971): 1449-1450.

characteristics, as well as the most appropriate manner of dealing with them, both in health and disease.

Several large cities in the United States already have special medical diagnostic centers into which information on the symptoms of a patient may be fed from individual hospitals or even individual doctors, and after being processed by a computer, a diagnosis is automatically transmitted to the user.

The greatest contributions of computerized medicine, however, will come from its focus on health, in contrast to the present focus of medicine on disease. It is a matter not simply of preventing disease, important as that is, but of enabling the individual to maintain and improve his health. For example, since the hereditary background of every individual will be known, a regimen can be provided for the individual so that he may be able to avoid all those conditions that might adversely affect him, and engage in all those that contribute to his health. We may, as a consequence, predict an enormous improvement in the health and longevity of the individual, and an accompanying comparable decrease in illness, disability, and death rates at all ages, with immeasureable benefit to the individual, his society, and humanity.

In medicine, as in virtually every other human enterprise, computers will not only improve the quality of medical services, but transform medicine itself. Without health, nothing is of much value. The health of the people is a society's most fundamental asset; hence, health education will become an indispensable part of every citizen's education, so that the understanding of structural, physiological, and health matters will not be any longer the exclusive monopoly of a particular profession, but will concern everyone. Professionals in various fields of health will be more competent than they are today because they will have received superior training in curricula tailored by a computer to the particular qualities of the individual. Thus, under such conditions, the future will include highly trained specialists, with every kind of other "ist" in between these two classes of professionals. The possibilities are really endless.

LOVE AND MARRIAGE

Computer dating has been in vogue for some years, but the future holds far greater possibilities for taking the element of chance out of marriage than it does even for dating. At the present time one out of two marriages in California ends in divorce, and in the remainder of the United States the figure approaches one out of three. Clearly, something is very wrong with the choice of criteria upon which so many Americans enter into marriage. Almost everyone who marries enters into the arrangement with the hope and expectation of permanency—a hope and expectation that is in far too many cases dashed upon the rock of "incompatibility." With the computer, we can do something about that. With the necessary information at its disposal, the computer can provide a specification of the risks or chance of any two individuals making or not making a go of it. The Marriage Consultation Agency can provide in a few minutes the advice sought that can prevent a lifetime of anguish.

It is known that the earlier the age of marriage the greater is the chance of divorce. Figures released by the Census Bureau in October 1971 show that within 20 years of marriage, 28 percent of the men who married before the age of 22 had been divorced, compared with 13 percent among men who had been married when they were older. The comparable findings for women were 27 percent compared with 14 percent of those who married later. So mother really does know better, but there can be little doubt that the computer would know better still.

In California, between 16 and 18 percent of the women who marry are pregnant when they do so. Better methods of birth control would undoubtedly greatly reduce the number of such marriages and the number of divorces that often follow such "shotgun" marriages.

Until human beings become infallible judges of human character, they would be well advised to accept a dispassionate analysis and judgment of anyone they are considering as a possible spouse. People who "fall" in love are in no condition to evaluate the qualities of the object of their "love," and only too often mistake an infatuation, a form of temporary insanity when the individual is least capable of governing his own affairs, and still less of assessing the character of the "loved" one. The computer will introduce a much-needed transformation from the spurious conception of "love" that leads to so many disastrous marriages, to a much more humane and reasonable basis for marriage that will hold far more hope for a genuine and enduring love.

In the matter of when and how many children a couple could most reasonably have, that is to say, with care and forethought for the welfare of the family as a whole, and of society in general, the computer can prove to be superior to any other source of advice, for with its reputation for soundness and dispassion, it can be more convincing than any strictly human agency.

In the adoption of children, again, the computer can perform the task of matching children to prospective parents and prospective parents to children more efficiently than could any other instrumentality. The adoption of children will altogether be put on a more efficient, more intelligent, and more humane basis than it is at present, since a central register of children available for adoption will make the task of locating the principal prospective parents and children a much easier, faster, and happier occasion for everyone.

The working week may, by the end of this century, quite possibly be reduced to four days and then to three days, and each working day may be up to several hours shorter than at present. Parents may be together with their children for the greater part of the time. The consequences of this will be of considerable benefit. The father will again participate in the bringing up of his children jointly with his wife, instead of being the absentee father that many married men have been forced to become under the conditions of contemporary life.

WILL THE EXTENDED FAMILY RETURN?

Because of a number of complex changes, greater industrialization, the flight from rural life to the city, and above all the automobile, the extended family of earlier days has given way to the nuclear family of just father and mother and children. Grandparents, uncles, aunts, and cousins, all living in their own nuclear families are likely to be separated from one another by hundreds of thousands of miles, and see each other so seldom that their contacts are minimal. This change in family structure constitutes yet another cause and effect of the atomization, the fragmentation of human relationships, that has overtaken contemporary man—and it is not a healthy or desirable condition. The variety of human relationships, the refuge and sympathy the extended family provided, the multiplicity of personalities, problems, angles of vision, protection, and community, constituted an amalgam of enriching humanity that is sadly lacking in the contemporary nuclear family. Where, formerly, the extended family contributed to the development of a personality that was outgoing and interested in extended relationships, the nuclear family contributes to the development of the very obverse of such a personality, a personality that is by contrast isolated, private, and insulated from others. This is not a happy development, and the revolt against the boredom, the aimlessness, and the discontent that such families tend to breed is evident in the ground swell of communalism among the young of those lands, and especially in the United States, in which the nuclear family has been dominant for more than two generations. There is a yearning for human relationships, the warmth, the sympathy, and the bonding that characterized the richness of the extended family in the past.

Will it be possible to return to the extended family? It will certainly be possible for vastly greater numbers of human beings than have enjoyed the experience during the last half century. This will necessitate not so much a reorganization of the family, as a reorganization of the community and the city. Here, too, the computer will play a principal role in the planning and organization of new communities and the reconstitution of the city. Will men ever return to the land, the rural life, to the small town, the community? It is a question that many men have been asking themselves, and some have given back the unequivocal answer that they, at least, will do so, by moving to the country or a small town, or buying and operating a small farm. Some have even left their homelands in order to escape from the city and live a more human life together with their families.

SUMMARY

All man's discoveries are ethically neutral. Man alone determines whether they are used for good or evil purposes. The story of Adam and Eve's eating the forbidden fruit makes this point. Innocent Adam was in danger of being unable to distinguish between the good and the evil fruit of the tree of knowledge and of accepting and worshiping evil as good; his punishment for this would be death. It seems that this parable has almost come to pass, because man has acquired so much knowledge without understanding that his knowledge threatens to destroy him. Mankind stands very near the edge of doom. With the power of the hydrogen bomb, and with the environmental damage that is increasingly destroying our vital resources of air, water, plants, and animals, who can doubt it?

If we continue to act as we have done in the past, we shall have only a past and no future. We must assume that human beings can and will change, that computers will play a revolutionary role in effecting changes—and, we hope, positive changes. The only philosophically tenable position, even for a pessimist in a time of crisis, is optimism. We must live and work as if our life and work may make the necessary difference, creating a world where, as we have said earlier, men live as if to live and love were one.

Index